Immigration Court Practice Manual

Table of Contents

Chapter 1 The Immigration Court

1.1   Scope of the Practice Manual

(a) Authority — The Executive Office for Immigration Review (EOIR) is charged with administering the immigration courts nationwide. The Attorney General has directed the Director of EOIR, in consultation with the immigration judges, to issue an Immigration Court Practice Manual.

(b) Purpose — EOIR provides this Practice Manual for the information and convenience of the general public and for parties that appear before the immigration courts. The manual describes procedures, requirements, and recommendations for practice before the immigration courts. The requirements set forth in this manual are binding on the parties who appear before the immigration courts, unless the immigration judge directs otherwise in a particular case.

(c) Disclaimer — This Practice Manual does not constitute legal advice, and no parties or members of the public should construe any provision as legal advice. This manual does not extend or limit the jurisdiction of the immigration courts as established by law and regulation. Nothing in this manual shall limit the discretion of immigration judges to act in accordance with law and regulation.

(d) Revisions — EOIR reserves the right to amend, suspend, or revoke the text, or portions of the text, of this Practice Manual at any time.

The most current version of the Practice Manual is available at the EOIR website. Questions regarding online access to the Practice Manual should be addressed to the Law Library and Immigration Research Center. See Appendix A (Directory).

The Practice Manual is updated periodically. Dates of the most recent updates to the practice manual are provided. Parties should make sure to consult the most recent version of the Practice Manual, which is posted online at the EOIR website.

For information on how to provide comments regarding this Practice Manual, see Chapter 13 (Public Input).

(e) Reproductions — The Practice Manual is a public document and may be reproduced without advance authorization from the Executive Office for Immigration Review.

1.2   Function of the Office of the Chief Immigration Judge

(a) Role — The Office of the Chief Immigration Judge oversees the administration of the immigration courts nationwide and exercises administrative supervision over immigration judges. Immigration judges are responsible for conducting immigration court proceedings and act independently in deciding matters before them. Immigration judges are tasked with resolving cases in a manner that is timely, impartial, and consistent with the Immigration and Nationality Act, federal regulations, and precedent decisions of the Board of Immigration Appeals and federal appellate courts.

(b) Location within the Federal Government — The Office of the Chief Immigration Judge (OCIJ) is a component of the Executive Office for Immigration Review (EOIR). Along with the Board of Immigration Appeals and the Office of the Chief Administrative Hearing Officer, OCIJ operates under the supervision of the Director of EOIR. See 8 C.F.R. § 1003.0(a). In turn, EOIR is a component of the Department of Justice and operates under the authority and supervision of the Attorney General. See Appendix B (Org Chart).

(c) Relationship to the Board of Immigration Appeals — The Board of Immigration Appeals (Board) is the highest administrative tribunal adjudicating immigration and nationality matters. The Board is responsible for applying the immigration and nationality laws uniformly throughout the United States. Accordingly, the Board has been given nationwide jurisdiction to review decisions of immigration judges and certain decisions made by the Department of Homeland Security (DHS). The Board is tasked with resolving the questions before it in a manner that is timely, impartial, and consistent with the Immigration and Nationality Act (INA) and federal regulations. The Board is also tasked with providing clear and uniform guidance to immigration judges, DHS, and the general public on the proper interpretation and administration of the INA and the federal regulations. See 8 C.F.R. § 1003.1(d)(1). See also Appendix B (Org Chart). Finally, the Board has authority over the disciplining and sanctioning of practitioners appearing before the immigration courts, DHS, and the Board and recognized organizations. See Chapter 10 (Discipline of Practitioners).

For detailed guidance on practice before the Board, parties should consult the Board of Immigration Appeals Practice Manual.

(d) Relationship to the Department of Homeland Security — The Department of Homeland Security (DHS) was created in 2003 and assumed most of the functions of the former Immigration and Naturalization Service. DHS is responsible for enforcing immigration laws and administering immigration and naturalization benefits. By contrast, the immigration courts and the Board of Immigration Appeals are responsible for independently adjudicating cases under the immigration laws. Thus, DHS is entirely separate from the Department of Justice and the Executive Office for Immigration Review. In proceedings before the immigration court or the Board, DHS is deemed to be a party and is represented by its component, U.S. Immigration and Customs Enforcement (ICE). See Chapters 1.4(a) (Jurisdiction), 1.4(c) (Immigration Judge Decisions), 1.4(e) (Department of Homeland Security).

(e) Relationship to the Immigration and Naturalization Service — Prior to the creation of the Department of Homeland Security (DHS), the Immigration and Naturalization Service (INS) was responsible for enforcing immigration laws and administering immigration and naturalization benefits. INS was a component of the Department of Justice. INS has been abolished and its role has been assumed by DHS, which is entirely separate from the Department of Justice. See subsection (d), above.

(f) Relationship to the Office of the Chief Administrative Hearing Officer — The Office of the Chief Administrative Hearing Officer (OCAHO) is an independent entity within the Executive Office for Immigration Review. OCAHO is responsible for hearings involving employer sanctions, anti-discrimination provisions, and document fraud under the Immigration and Nationality Act. OCAHO's Administrative Law Judges are not affiliated with the Office of the Chief Immigration Judge. The Board of Immigration Appeals does not review OCAHO decisions. See Appendix B (Org Chart).

(g) Relationship to the Administrative Appeals Office — The Administrative Appeals Office (AAO), sometimes referred to as the Administrative Appeals Unit (AAU), was a component of the former Immigration and Naturalization Service and is now a component of the Department of Homeland Security (DHS). The AAO adjudicates appeals from DHS denials of certain kinds of applications and petitions, including employment-based immigrant petitions and most nonimmigrant visa petitions. See 8 C.F.R. §§ 103.2, 103.3. The AAO is not a component of the Department of Justice. The AAO should not be confused with the Executive Office for Immigration Review, the Office of the Chief Immigration Judge, or the Board of Immigration Appeals. See Appendix B (Org Chart).

(h) Relationship to the Office of Immigration Litigation (OIL) — The Office of Immigration Litigation (OIL) represents the United States government in immigration-related civil trial litigation and appellate litigation in the federal courts. OIL is a component of the Department of Justice, located in the Civil Division. OIL is separate and distinct from the Executive Office for Immigration Review (EOIR). OIL should not be confused with EOIR, the Office of the Chief Immigration Judge, or the Board of Immigration Appeals. See Appendix B (Org Chart).

1.3   Composition of the Office of the Chief Immigration Judge

(a) General — The Office of the Chief Immigration Judge (OCIJ) supervises and directs the activities of the immigration courts. OCIJ operates under the supervision of the Director of the Executive Office for Immigration Review (EOIR). OCIJ develops operating policies for the immigration courts, oversees policy implementation, evaluates the performance of the immigration courts, and provides overall supervision of the immigration judges.

(1) Chief Immigration Judge — The Chief Immigration Judge (CIJ) oversees the administration of the immigration courts nationwide.

(2) Principal Deputy Chief Immigration Judge — The Principal Deputy Chief Immigration Judge (PDCIJ) assists the CIJ in overseeing the administration of the immigration courts throughout the country and supervises the Regional Deputy Chief Immigration Judges.

(3) Regional Deputy Chief Immigration Judges — The Regional Deputy Chief Immigration Judges (RDCIJs) assist the PDCIJ in carrying out the responsibilities of that office and are responsible for daily supervision of the Assistant Chief Immigration Judges (ACIJs) within the RDCIJs' assigned geographical regions.

(4) Assistant Chief Immigration Judges — The ACIJs oversee the operations of specific immigration courts. A listing of the immigration courts overseen by each ACIJ and assigned areas of responsibility is available on the EOIR website.

(5) Legal Staff: Chief Counsel and Attorney Advisors/Judicial Law Clerks — OCIJ has a sizable legal staff, which includes a chief counsel, attorneys at the OCIJ headquarters, and permanent and term attorney advisors and judicial law clerks (JLCs) at the immigration courts nationwide. The legal staff supports the CIJ, PDCIJ, RDCIJs, ACIJs, and immigration judges.

(6) Language Services Unit — The Language Services Unit (LSU) oversees staff interpreters and contract interpreters at the immigration courts. The LSU conducts quality assurance programs for all interpreters.

(b) Immigration Courts — EOIR employs immigration judges and professional staff in the immigration courts nationwide. As a general matter, immigration judges determine removability and adjudicate applications for relief or protection from removal. For the specific duties of immigration judges, see Chapter 1.4 (Jurisdiction and Authority). Immigration judge decisions are final unless timely appealed or certified to the BIA. See Chapter 6 (Appeals of Immigration Judge Decisions).

Court administrators are assigned to the local office of each immigration court. Under the supervision of an Assistant Chief Immigration Judge, the court administrator manages the daily activities of the immigration court and supervises staff interpreters, legal assistants, and clerical and technical employees.

In each immigration court, the court administrator serves as the liaison with the local office of the Department of Homeland Security, the private bar, and nonprofit organizations that represent noncitizens.

A listing of the immigration courts is available on the EOIR website.

(c) Immigration Judge Conduct and Professionalism — Immigration judges strive to act honorably, fairly, and in accordance with the highest ethical standards, thereby ensuring public confidence in the integrity and impartiality of immigration court proceedings. Alleged misconduct by immigration judges is taken seriously by the Department of Justice and the Executive Office for Immigration Review (EOIR), especially if it impugns the integrity of the hearing process.

Usually, when a disagreement arises with an immigration judge's ruling, the disagreement is properly raised in a motion to the immigration judge or an appeal to the Board of Immigration Appeals. When a party has an immediate concern regarding an immigration judge's conduct that is not appropriate for a motion or appeal, the concern may be raised with the Assistant Chief Immigration Judge (ACIJ) responsible for the court. Contact information for ACIJs is available on the EOIR website.

In the alternative, parties may raise concerns regarding an immigration judge's conduct directly with the Office of the Director by following the procedures outlined on the or by sending an email to: judicial.conduct@usdoj.gov. Where appropriate, concerns may also be raised with the Department of Justice, Office of Professional

Responsibility. All concerns, and any actions taken, may be considered confidential and not subject to disclosure.

1.4   Jurisdiction and Authority

(a) Jurisdiction — Immigration judges generally have the authority to:

- Make determinations of removability, deportability, and excludability

- Adjudicate applications for relief from removal or deportation, including, but not limited to, asylum, withholding of removal ("restriction on removal"), protection under the Convention Against Torture, cancellation of removal, adjustment of status, registry, and certain waivers

- Review credible fear and reasonable fear determinations made by the Department of Homeland Security (DHS)

- Conduct claimed status review proceedings

- Conduct custody hearings and bond redetermination proceedings

- Make determinations in rescission of adjustment of status and departure control cases

- Take any other action consistent with applicable law and regulation as may be appropriate, including such actions as ruling on motions, issuing subpoenas, and ordering pre-hearing conferences and statements

- Conduct disciplinary proceedings pertaining to practitioners, as discussed in Chapter 10 (Discipline of Practitioners)

- Administer the oath of citizenship in administrative naturalization ceremonies conducted by DHS

- Conduct removal proceedings initiated by the Office of Special Investigations

See 8 C.F.R. §§ 1240.1(a), 1240.31, 1240.41.

(b) No Jurisdiction — Although immigration judges exercise broad authority over matters brought before the immigration courts, there are certain immigration-related matters over which immigration judges do not have authority, such as:

- Visa petitions

- Employment authorization

- Certain waivers

- Naturalization applications

- Revocation of naturalization

- Parole into the United States under INA § 212(d)(5)

- Applications for advance parole
- Employer sanctions
- Administrative fines and penalties under 8 C.F.R. parts 280 and 1280
- Determinations by the Department of Homeland Security involving safe third country agreements

See 8 C.F.R. §§ 103.2, 1003.42(h), 28 C.F.R. § 68.26.

(c) Immigration Judge Decisions — Immigration judges render oral and written decisions at the end of immigration court proceedings. See Chapter 4.16(g) (Decision). A decision of an immigration judge is final unless a party timely appeals the decision to the Board of Immigration Appeals or the case is certified to the Board. Parties should note that the certification of a case is separate from any appeal in the case. See Chapter 6 (Appeals of Immigration Judge Decisions).

(d) Board of Immigration Appeals — The Board of Immigration Appeals has broad authority to review the decisions of immigration judges. See 8 C.F.R. § 1003.1(b). See also Chapter 6 (Appeals of Immigration Judge Decisions). Although the immigration courts and the Board are both components of the Executive Office for Immigration Review, the two are separate and distinct entities. Thus, administrative supervision of Board Members is vested in the Chairman of the Board, not the Office of the Chief Immigration Judge. See Chapter 1.2(c) (Relationship to the Board of Immigration Appeals); see also Appendix B (Org Chart).

(e) Department of Homeland Security — The Department of Homeland Security (DHS) enforces the immigration and nationality laws and represents the United States government's interests in immigration proceedings. DHS also adjudicates visa petitions and applications for immigration benefits. See, e.g., 8 C.F.R. § 1003.1(b)(4), (5). DHS is entirely separate from the Department of Justice and the Executive Office for Immigration Review. When appearing before an immigration court, DHS is deemed a party to the proceedings and is represented by its component, U.S. Immigration and Customs Enforcement (ICE). See Chapter 1.2(d) (Relationship to the Department of Homeland Security)

(f) Attorney General — Decisions of immigration judges are reviewable by the Board of Immigration Appeals. The Board's decisions may be referred to the Attorney General for review. Referral may occur at the Attorney General's request, or at the request of the Department of Homeland Security or the Board. The Attorney General may vacate any decision of the Board and issue their own decision in its place. See 8 C.F.R. § 1003.1(d)(1)(i), (h). Decisions of the Attorney General may be published as precedent decisions. The Attorney General's precedent decisions appear with the Board's precedent decisions in Administrative Decisions Under Immigration and Nationality Law of the United States ("I&N Decisions").

(g) Federal Courts — Decisions of immigration judges are reviewable by the Board of Immigration Appeals. In turn, decisions of the Board are reviewable in certain federal courts, depending on the nature of the appeal. When a decision of the Board is reviewed by a federal court, the Board provides that court with a certified copy of the record before the Board. This record includes the Record of Proceedings before the immigration judge.

1.5   Public Access

(a) Court Locations

(1) Office of the Chief Immigration Judge — The Office of the Chief Immigration Judge, which oversees the administration of the immigration courts nationwide, is located at the Executive Office for Immigration Review headquarters in Falls Church, Virginia. See Appendix A (Directory).

(2) Hearing locations — There are more than 500 immigration judges in more than 60 immigration courts in the United States. A list of immigration courts is available in Appendix A (Directory), as well as on the EOIR website.

Immigration judges sometimes hold hearings in alternate locations, such as designated detail cities where the caseload is significant but inadequate to warrant the establishment of a permanent immigration court. Immigration judges also conduct hearings in Department of Homeland Security detention centers nationwide, as well as many federal, state, and local correctional facilities. Documents pertaining to hearings held in these locations are filed at the appropriate administrative control court. See Chapter 3.1(a)(1) (Administrative control courts).

In addition, hearings before immigration judges are sometimes conducted by video conference or, under certain conditions, by telephone conference. See Chapter 4.7 (Hearings by Video or Telephone Conference).

With certain exceptions, hearings before immigration judges are open to the public. See Chapter 4.9 (Public Access). The public's access to immigration hearings is discussed in Chapter 4.14 (Access to Court). For additional information on the conduct of hearings, see Chapters 4.12 (Courtroom Decorum), 4.13 (Electronic Devices).

(b) Library and Online Resources —

(1) Law Library and Immigration Research Center — The Office of Policy, Communications and Legislative Affairs Division, maintains a Law Library and Immigration Research Center (LLIRC) at 5107 Leesburg Pike, Suite 1800, Falls Church, Virginia 22041. The LLIRC maintains select sources of immigration law, including Board decisions, federal statutes and regulations, federal case reporters, immigration law treatises, and various secondary sources. The LLIRC serves the Executive Office for Immigration Review (EOIR), including the Office of the Chief Immigration Judge and the immigration courts, as well as the general public. For hours of operation, directions, and collection information, contact the LLIRC at (703) 605-1103 or visit the EOIR website. See Appendix A (Directory).

The LLIRC is not a lending library, and all printed materials must be reviewed on the premises. LLIRC staff may assist patrons in locating materials but are not available for research assistance. LLIRC staff do not provide legal advice or guidance regarding filing or procedures for matters before the immigration courts. LLIRC staff may, however, provide guidance in locating published decisions of the Board.

Limited self-service copying is available in the LLIRC.

(2) Virtual Law Library — The LLIRC maintains a "Virtual Law Library," accessible on the EOIR website. The Virtual Law Library serves as a comprehensive repository of immigration-related law and information for use by the general public.

(3) Immigration Court Online Resource — The Immigration Court Online Resource (ICOR) is a centralized location for resources and information about immigration proceedings before the Executive Office for Immigration Review (EOIR). The ICOR is available on EOIR's website at https://icor.eoir.usdoj.gov.

(c) Records —

(1) Inspection by parties — Parties to a proceeding, and their practitioners of record, may inspect the official records of proceedings. A FOIA request is not required. Inspection by prior arrangement with court staff is strongly recommended to ensure that the official record of proceedings is immediately available. Individual immigration courts can be reached by using the following email model: "EOIR.xyz.ROP.Requests@usdoj.gov" where the "xyz" represents the relevant immigration court's three-letter code. See Appendix Q (Immigration Court Three Letter Codes). Parties may review all portions of the record that are not prohibited (e.g., classified information, documents under a protective order). EOIR prohibits the removal of official records by parties or other persons from EOIR-controlled space.

(2) Inspection by non-parties — Persons or entities who are not a party to a proceeding must file a request for information pursuant to the Freedom of Information Act (FOIA) to inspect the Record of Proceedings. See Chapter 12 (Requesting Records).

(3) Copies for parties — The immigration court will provide copies of the official record of proceedings to parties and their practitioners of record upon request. A FOIA request is not required. Parties may obtain a copy of all portions of the record that are not prohibited (e.g., classified information, documents under a protective order). Requests for copies of the official record of proceedings may be made to the immigration courts in person, by mail, or via email. See email address model in Chapter 1.5(c)(1) (Inspection by parties). The immigration courts do not provide self-service copying. Alternatively, the parties may file a request for information pursuant to the Freedom of Information Act (FOIA). See Chapter 12 (Requesting Records).

(4) Audio recordings — Immigration judges previously recorded immigration court hearings on cassette tapes and now record immigration court hearings digitally. The court will provide a copy of the hearing recording in digital format at the request of a party.

(5) Copies for non-parties — Persons who are not a party to a proceeding must file a FOIA request with the EOIR Office of General Counsel if they wish to see or obtain copies of the record of proceeding. See Chapter 12 (Requesting Records).

(6) Confidentiality — The immigration courts take special precautions to ensure the confidentiality of cases involving noncitizens in exclusion proceedings, asylum applicants, battered noncitizen spouses and children, classified information, and information subject to a protective order.

(7) Electronic records — For cases with electronic records of proceeding (eROPs), eligible parties may view and download the eROP through the EOIR Courts & Appeals System (ECAS).

1.6   Inquiries

(a) Generally — All inquiries to an immigration court must contain or provide the following information for each respondent:

- Complete name (as it appears on the charging document)

- A-number

- Type of proceeding (removal, deportation, exclusion, bond, etc.)

- Date of the upcoming master calendar or individual calendar hearing

- The completion date, if the court proceedings have been completed

See also Chapter 3.3(c)(6) (Cover page and caption), Appendix E (Cover Pages).

(b) Press Inquiries — All inquiries from the press should be directed to the Executive Office for Immigration Review, Office of Policy, Communications and Legislative Affairs Division. For contact information, see Appendix A (Directory).

(c) Automated Case Information Hotline — The Automated Case Information Hotline provides information about the status of cases before an immigration court or the Board of Immigration Appeals. See Appendix A (Directory), Appendix H (Hotlines). The Automated Case Information Hotline contains a telephone menu (in English and Spanish) covering most kinds of cases. The caller must enter the A-number of the noncitizen involved. A-numbers have nine digits (e.g., A 234 567 890). Formerly, A-numbers had eight digits (e.g., A 12 345 678). In the case of an eight-digit A-number, the caller should enter a "0" before the A-number (e.g., A 012 345 678).

(1) Immigration court — The Automated Case Information Hotline contains information regarding:

- The next hearing date, time, and location

- In asylum cases, the elapsed time and status of the asylum EAD clock

- Immigration judge decisions

The Automated Case Information Hotline does not contain information regarding:

- Bond proceedings

- Motions

(2) Additional inquiries — Inquiries that cannot be answered by the Automated Case Information Hotline may be directed to the immigration court in which the proceedings are pending or to the appropriate administrative control court. See Chapter 3.1(a)(1) (Administrative control courts). Callers must be aware that court administrators and other staff members are prohibited from providing any legal advice and that no information provided by court administrators or other staff members may be construed as legal advice.

(d) Inquiries to Immigration Court Staff — Most questions regarding immigration court proceedings can be answered through the automated telephone number, known as the Automated Case Information Hotline. See subsection (c), above. For other questions, telephone inquiries may be made to immigration court staff. Collect calls are not accepted.

If a telephone inquiry cannot be answered by immigration court staff, the caller may be advised to submit an inquiry in writing, with a copy served on the opposing party. See Appendix A (Directory).

In addition, court administrators and other staff members cannot provide legal advice to parties.

(e) Inquiries to Specific Immigration Judges — Callers must bear in mind that immigration judges cannot engage in ex parte communications. A party cannot speak about a case with the immigration judge when the other party is not present, and all written communications about a case must be served on the opposing party.

(f) Faxes — Immigration courts generally do not accept inquiries by fax. See Chapter 3.1(a)(7) (Faxes).

(g) Electronic Communications —

(1) Internet — The Executive Office for Immigration Review (EOIR) maintains a website at www.justice.gov/eoir. See Appendix A (Directory). The website contains information about the immigration courts, the Office of the Chief Immigration Judge, the Board of Immigration Appeals, and the other components of EOIR. It also contains newly published regulations, the Board's precedent decisions, and a copy of this manual. See Chapter 1.5(b) (Library and Online Resources).

(2) Email — Immigration courts generally do not accept case related inquiries by email.

(3) EOIR Courts & Appeals System (ECAS) — ECAS is a suite of EOIR web-based applications that allows attorneys and fully accredited representatives to electronically register with EOIR, access case information and hearing calendars, as well as electronically file documents and view eROPs in eligible cases. Similarly, these web-based applications provide access for authorized DHS users. Access to these applications is available on EOIR's website at https://www.justice.gov/eoir/ECAS.

(4) Electronic Registry (eRegistry) — Attorneys and fully accredited representatives who are accredited to appear before EOIR must electronically register with EOIR eRegistry through ECAS in order to practice before the immigration courts and to use ECAS. eRegistry is the online process that is used to electronically register with EOIR. See Chapter 2.3(a)(1) (eRegistry), 2.4 (Accredited Representatives and Recognized Organizations).

(5) Automated Case Information system — The Automated Case Information system (ACIS) provides information about the status of cases (in English and Spanish) before immigration judges and the Board. The information on ACIS is similar to the information provided by telephone via the Automated Case Information Hotline. See Chapter 1.6(c) (Automated Case Information Hotline). Access to ACIS is available on EOIR's website at https://acis.eoir.justice.gov/.

(h) Emergencies and Requests to Advance Hearing Dates — If circumstances require urgent action by an immigration judge, parties should follow the procedures set forth in Chapters 5.10(b) (Motion to Advance) or 8 (Stays), as appropriate.

This page intentionally left blank.

Chapter 2 Appearances before the Immigration Court

2.1 Representation and Appearances Generally

(a) Right to Counsel and Individuals Authorized to Provide Representation and Make Appearances — Under the regulations, parties appearing before the immigration court may represent themselves (Chapter 2.2) or be represented by practitioners. See 8 C.F.R. §§ 1001.1(ff), 1292.1. Practitioners include: attorneys (Chapter 2.3), accredited representatives (Chapter 2.4), and certain categories of persons who are expressly recognized by the immigration court (Chapters 2.5, 2.8, and 2.9).

A respondent may be represented by a practitioner of their choosing, at no cost to the government. As in most civil or administrative proceedings, the government does not provide legal counsel. The immigration court provides respondents with a list of pro bono legal service providers who may be willing to represent respondents at no cost. Many of these providers may represent respondents on appeal as well. See Chapter 2.2(b) (List of Pro Bono Legal Service Providers). Bar associations and nonprofit agencies can also refer noncitizens to practitioners.

Attorneys and accredited representatives must register with EOIR in order to practice before the immigration court. See 8 C.F.R. § 1292.1(a)(1), (a)(4), (f); Chapters 2.3(a)(1) (eRegistry), 2.4 (Accredited Representatives and Recognized Organizations). Other practitioners are not required to register with EOIR.

No one other than a practitioner is authorized to appear before the immigration court. Non-lawyer immigration specialists, visa consultants, and "notarios" are *not* authorized to represent parties or appear before the immigration court.

(b) Entering an Appearance as the Practitioner of Record — To perform the functions of and become the practitioner of record, a practitioner must file a Notice of Entry of Appearance as Attorney or Representative Before the Immigration Court (Form EOIR-28). A practitioner of record is authorized and required to appear on behalf of a respondent, to file all documents on behalf of a respondent, and to accept service of process of all documents filed in the proceedings. A properly filed Form EOIR-28 provides a practitioner with access to the record of proceedings during the course of proceedings. A respondent is considered to be represented for the proceeding in which a Form EOIR-28 has been properly filed and accepted. See 8 C.F.R. §§ 1003.17, 1292.4, 1292.5(a).

Note that different forms are used to enter an appearance before an immigration court, the Board of Immigration Appeals, and the Department of Homeland Security (DHS). The forms used to enter an appearance before the Board and DHS are as follows:

- The Notice of Entry of Appearance as Attorney or Representative Before the Board of Immigration Appeals (Form EOIR-27) is used to enter an appearance as the practitioner of record before the Board

- The Notice of Entry of Appearance of Attorney or Representative (Form G-28) is used to enter an appearance before DHS

The immigration court will not recognize a practitioner as the practitioner of record using any form except the Form EOIR-28. Persons representing themselves ("pro se") should not file a Form EOIR-28.

(1) How to File the Form EOIR-28 —

(A) Electronic Entry of Appearance — After registering with EOIR's eRegistry, attorneys and accredited representatives must electronically file the Form EOIR- 28 through ECAS in the following situations:

- The first appearance of the attorney or accredited representative, either at a hearing or by filing a pleading, motion, application, or other document

- Whenever a case is remanded to the immigration court

- Any change of business address or telephone number for the attorney or accredited representative

- Upon reinstatement following the suspension or disbarment of an attorney or accredited representative from practice

(B) Paper Entry of Appearance — Practitioners who are neither attorneys nor accredited representatives must file a paper Form EOIR-28 in all circumstances. Additionally, a paper, and not an electronic, Form EOIR-28 must be filed by all practitioners in the following situations:

- A motion to recalendar proceedings that are administratively closed

- Disciplinary proceedings

When filing a paper Form EOIR-28, practitioners should be sure to use the most current version of the form, which can be found on the EOIR website. See also Chapter 11 (Forms), Appendix D (Forms). The use of green paper when filing a paper Form EOIR-28 is strongly encouraged. See Chapter 11.2(f) (Form Colors).

If a paper Form EOIR-28 is submitted with other documents, the Form EOIR-28 should be at the front of the package. See Chapter 3.3(c) (Format). It should *not* be included as an exhibit, as part of an exhibit, or with other supporting materials.

(C) Notice to Opposing Party — Where the Form EOIR-28 cannot be filed electronically through ECAS, DHS must be served with a paper copy of the Form EOIR-28 when it is filed with the immigration court. See Chapter 3.2 (Service on the Opposing Party).

(2) Scope of Representation — When completing the Form EOIR-28, a practitioner must check the box indicating whether the entry of appearance is for all proceedings, custody and bond proceedings only, or all proceedings other than custody and bond proceedings. Once a practitioner has made an appearance, that practitioner has an obligation to continue representation until such time as a motion to withdraw or substitute counsel has been granted by the immigration court. See Chapter 2.1(b)(3) (Change in Representation).

(3) Change in Representation — When a practitioner wishes to change the scope of their appearance in a particular case, the practitioner must file a new Form EOIR-28 and, if necessary, a motion to withdraw or substitute counsel. Changes in representation may be made as described below.

(A) Change in Scope of Representation — If a practitioner wishes to change the scope of representation indicated on a previously filed Form EOIR-28 to either increase or decrease the scope of representation but not completely withdraw from the representation, the practitioner must file a new Form EOIR-28 and, as applicable, a motion to withdraw. For example:

- If a practitioner previously filed a Form EOIR-28 and checked the box indicating that the entry of appearance is for custody and bond proceedings only, and the practitioners later wishes to represent the same respondent in removal proceedings as well, the practitioner must file a new Form EOIR-28 and check the box indicating that the entry of appearance is for all proceedings or removal proceedings, as appropriate.

- If a practitioner previously filed a Form EOIR-28 and checked the box indicating that the entry of appearance is for all proceedings, and the practitioner later no longer wishes to represent the respondent in removal proceedings but does wish to continue representing the respondent in custody and bond proceedings only, the practitioner must file a motion to withdraw from the removal proceedings as well as a new Form EOIR-28 in which the practitioner has checked the box indicating that the entry of appearance is for custody and bond proceedings only.

(B) Substitution of counsel — When a respondent wishes to substitute a new practitioner for a previous practitioner, the new practitioner must submit a written or oral motion for substitution of counsel, accompanied by a Form EOIR-28. See 8 C.F.R. § 1003.17(a)(3). If in writing, the motion should be filed with a cover page labeled "MOTION FOR SUBSTITUTION OF COUNSEL" and comply with the deadlines and requirements for filing. See Chapter 3 (Filing with the Immigration Court), Appendix E (Cover Pages). The motion should contain the following information:

- whether the motion to substitute counsel is for all proceedings, custody and bond proceedings only, or all proceedings other than custody and bond proceeding

- the reason(s) for the substitution of counsel, in conformance with applicable state bar and other ethical rules

- evidence that the prior practitioner has been notified about the motion for substitution of counsel

- evidence of the respondent's consent to the substitution of counsel

If the motion is in writing, the new practitioner should serve a copy of the motion and executed Form EOIR-28 on the prior practitioner, as well as on the Department of Homeland Security If required. A Proof of Service of the motion and Form EOIR-28 on the prior practitioner is sufficient to show that the prior practitioner has been notified about the motion to substitute counsel.

In adjudicating a motion for substitution of counsel, the time remaining before the next hearing and the reason(s) given for the substitution are taken into consideration. Extension requests based on substitution of counsel are not favored.

If a motion for substitution of counsel is granted, the prior practitioner need not file a motion to withdraw. However, until a motion for substitution of counsel is granted, the original practitioner remains the respondent's practitioner of record and must appear at all scheduled hearings.

The granting of a motion for substitution of counsel does *not* constitute a continuance of a scheduled hearing. Accordingly, parties must be prepared to proceed at the next scheduled hearing.

(C) Withdrawal of counsel — When a practitioner wishes to withdraw from representing a respondent, the practitioner must submit a written or oral motion to withdraw. See 8 C.F.R. § 1003.17(b). If in writing, the motion should be filed with a cover page labeled "MOTION TO WITHDRAW AS COUNSEL" and comply with the deadlines and requirements for filing. See Chapter 3 (Filing with the Immigration Court), Appendix E (Cover Pages). The motion should contain the following information:

- whether the motion to withdraw is for all proceedings, custody and bond proceedings only, or all proceedings other than custody and bond proceedings

- the reason(s) for the withdrawal of counsel, in conformance with applicable state bar or other ethical rules

- the last known address of the respondent

- a statement that the practitioner has notified the respondent of the request to withdraw as counsel or, if the respondent could not be notified, an explanation of the efforts made to notify the respondent of the request

- evidence of the respondent's consent to withdraw or a statement of why evidence of such consent is unobtainable

- evidence that the practitioner notified or attempted to notify the respondent, with a recitation of specific efforts made, of (a) pending deadlines; (b) the date, time, and place of the next scheduled hearing; (c) the necessity of meeting deadlines and appearing at scheduled hearings; and (d) the consequences of failing to meet deadlines or appear at scheduled hearings

In adjudicating a motion to withdraw, the time remaining before the next hearing and the reason(s) given for the withdrawal are taken into consideration.

Until a motion to withdraw is granted, the practitioner who filed the motion remains the practitioner of record and must attend all scheduled hearings.

(D) Release of counsel/practitioner — When a respondent elects to terminate representation by a practitioner, the practitioner remains the practitioner of record until the immigration judge has granted either a motion for substitution of counsel or a motion to withdraw, as appropriate. See (B) and (C), above.

(4) Multiple Practitioners — Sometimes, a respondent may retain more than one practitioner at a time. In such cases, *all* of the practitioners are practitioners of record, and will all be held responsible as practitioners for the respondent. One of the practitioners is recognized as the primary practitioner (notice attorney). All of the practitioners must file a Form EOIR-28, checking the appropriate box to reflect whether the practitioner is the primary practitioner or a non-primary practitioner. All submissions to the immigration court must bear the name of one of the practitioners of record and be signed by that practitioner. See Chapter 3.3(b) (Signatures).

(5) Law Firms/Organizations — Only individual practitioners, and not firms, offices, or organizations, may enter an appearance before the immigration court to act as a practitioner of record. Accordingly, the immigration court does not recognize appearances or accept pleadings, motions, briefs, or other filings submitted by a law firm, law office, or other entity if the name and signature of a practitioner of record is not included. See (4), above. See also Chapter 3.3(b)(2) (Law firms). If, at any time, more than one practitioner represents a respondent, one of the practitioners must be designated as the primary practitioner (notice practitioner). See (4), above.

(A) Change in firm/organization — In the event that a practitioner departs a law firm or organization but wishes to continue representing the respondent as the practitioner of record, the practitioner must promptly file a new Form EOIR-28. The new Form EOIR-28 must reflect any change of address information and apprise the immigration court of their change in affiliation. The practitioner should check the "new address" box in the address block of the new Form EOIR-28, which must be served on the opposing party if not filed through ECAS. See Chapter 3.2 (Service on the Opposing Party).

(B) Change in practitioner — If the practitioner of record leaves a law firm/organization but the law firm/organization wishes to retain the case, another practitioner in the firm/organization must file a motion for substitution of counsel. Similarly, if a law firm/organization wishes to reassign responsibility for a case from one practitioner to another practitioner in the firm/organization, the new practitioner must file a motion for substitution of counsel. Until such time as a motion for substitution of counsel is granted, the original practitioner remains the respondent's practitioner of record and is responsible for the case. See (3), above.

(6) Address Obligations of Practitioners — All practitioners have an affirmative duty to keep the immigration court apprised of their current contact information, including address, email address, and telephone number. Changes in an attorney's or an accredited representative's address or contact information should be made by updating the registration information in the EOIR eRegistry to include the new address and contact information. See Chapter 2.3(a)(1) (eRegistry), 2.4 (Accredited Representatives and Recognized Organizations). However, updates to the registration in EOIR's eRegistry do not change an attorney's or an accredited representative's address in individual cases.

For practitioners of record, the practitioner must submit a new Form EOIR-28 for each respondent for which the practitioner's address is being changed. If a practitioner has multiple addresses, the practitioner should make sure that the appropriate practitioner address is designated for each respondent. See Chapter 2.3(b) (Appearances). The practitioner also should check the "New Address" box in the address block on the Form EOIR-28. The practitioner should *not* submit a change of address form (Form EOIR-33/IC) to notify the immigration court of a change in the practitioner's address.

(A) No compound changes of address — A practitioner of record may not simply submit a list of clients for whom their change of address should be entered. Practitioners of record must submit a new Form EOIR-28 for each represented respondent.

(B) Address obligations of represented respondents — Even when a respondent is represented by a practitioner of record, the respondent is still responsible for keeping the immigration court apprised of their address and telephone number. Address changes by practitioners of record on behalf of their clients must be submitted through the CASE Portal. Changes of address or telephone number for the respondent may not be made on the Form EOIR-28 but must be made on the change of address form (Form EOIR-33/IC). See Chapter 2.2(c) (Address Obligations).

(7) Filing After Entry of Appearance as Practitioner of Record — After a practitioner has filed a Form EOIR-28 and become the practitioner of record, all filings and communications to the immigration court must be submitted through the practitioner of record in accordance with EOIR filing polices. See 8 C.F.R. §§ 1003.17(a)(2), 1292.5(a); Chapter 3.1 (Delivery and Receipt).

(8) Appearances "on behalf of" — Appearances "on behalf of" occur when a second practitioner appears on behalf of the practitioner of record at a specific hearing before the immigration court. The practitioner making the appearance need not work at the same firm or organization as the practitioner of record. Appearances "on behalf of" are permitted as described below.

- First, the practitioner making the appearance must notify the immigration judge on the record that they are appearing on behalf of the practitioner of record.

- Second, the practitioner making the appearance must file a Notice of Entry of Appearance of Attorney or Representative Before the Immigration Court (Form EOIR-28) with the immigration court and serve it on the opposing party. The practitioner must file a paper Form EOIR-28, not an electronic Form EOIR-28. See Chapter 2.1(b)(1) (How to File the Form EOIR-28). The practitioner must check the box on the Form EOIR-28 indicating that they are making an appearance on behalf of the practitioner of record and fill in the name of the practitioner of record.

- Third, the appearance on behalf of the practitioner of record must be authorized by the immigration judge.

At the hearing, the practitioner making the appearance may file documents on behalf of the respondent. The practitioner making the appearance cannot file documents on behalf of the respondent at any other time. See Chapters 3.3(b) (Signatures), 3.2 (Service on the Opposing Party). The practitioner of record need not file a new Form EOIR-28 after the hearing.

(c) Limited Appearance for Document Assistance — Practitioners who have not filed a Form EOIR-28 to become the practitioner of record as discussed in (b), above, and who provide assistance to pro se respondents with the drafting, completion, or filling in of blank spaces of a specific motion, brief, form, or other document or set of documents intended to be filed with the immigration court, must disclose such assistance by completing a Notice of Entry of Limited Appearance for Document Assistance Before the Immigration Court (Form EOIR-61). In contrast to a practitioner of record, a practitioner who provides document assistance and discloses that assistance on a Form EOIR-61 does not have any ongoing obligations to the pro se respondent or the immigration court, if and when the Form EOIR-61 and the associated assisted documents are filed with the immigration court. A practitioner who enters a limited appearance is not authorized or required to appear in immigration court on behalf of respondent, is not authorized to have access to the record of proceedings, and is not required file a motion to withdraw. A respondent who receives document assistance is not represented, remains pro se, and is subject to service of process of all documents filed in the proceedings. See 8 C.F.R. §§ 1003.17(b), 1292.5.

(1) Filing Form EOIR-61 and Assisted Documents — The Form EOIR-61 is not filed as a standalone document and must be paper-filed at the same time as the document or set of documents with which the practitioner assisted. See 8 C.F.R. § 1003.17(b)(1).

Practitioners should use the most current version of the Form EOIR-61, which can be found on EOIR's website. See also Chapter 11 (Forms), Appendix D (Forms).

The Form EOIR-61 and assisted document or set of documents may be filed by the pro se respondent, or the pro se respondent may arrange for another individual, such as the practitioner who assisted, to file the documents in accordance with EOIR filing polices. See Chapter 3.1 (Delivery and Receipt). A Form EOIR-61 will not be accepted if a respondent has a practitioner of record in the relevant proceeding.

After the filing of a Form EOIR-61 and assisted document(s), any subsequent filing of an assisted document or set of documents must be accompanied by a new Form EOIR-61 from the practitioner, regardless of whether the same practitioner is providing assistance. See 8 C.F.R. § 1003.17(b)(1).

(2) Practitioner Identification on Assisted Documents — Notwithstanding a practitioner's disclosure of assistance on a Form EOIR-61, the practitioner must comply with the particular disclosure requirements for preparers on applications and forms, and the practitioner must identify themselves by name, accompanied by their signature, on motions, briefs, or other documents intended to be filed with the immigration court pursuant to a limited appearance for document assistance. See 8 C.F.R. § 1003.17(c).

2.2   Unrepresented Respondents ("Pro se" Appearances)

(a) Generally — Individuals in proceedings may represent themselves before the immigration court.

Individuals may choose to be represented by a practitioner of record for all or part of their proceedings before the immigration court or to receive document assistance from a practitioner. Due to the complexity of the immigration and nationality laws, the Office of the Chief Immigration Judge recommends that those who can obtain qualified professional representation or document assistance from a practitioner do so. See Chapters 2.3(a) (Qualifications), 2.4 (Accredited Representatives and Recognized Organizations), 2.5 (Law Students and Law Graduates).

(b) List of Pro Bono Legal Service Providers — The immigration courts cannot give advice regarding the selection of a practitioner. However, individuals in proceedings before an immigration court are provided with a list of pro bono legal service providers (the "List") within the region in which the immigration court is located. See 8 C.F.R. § 1003.61(a). The List is maintained by the Executive Office for Immigration Review, Legal Access Programs and contains information on non-profit organizations, referral services, and attorneys willing to provide pro bono legal services to individuals in immigration court proceedings. Providers appearing on the List may not be able to represent every individual who requests assistance.

In addition, all of the lists of pro bono legal service providers nationwide are available on the EOIR website.

(c) Address Obligations — Whether represented or not, respondents in proceedings before the immigration court must notify the immigration court within 5 days of any change in address or telephone number, using the change of address form (Form EOIR-33/IC). See 8 C.F.R. § 1003.15(d)(2). In many instances, the immigration court will send notification as to the time, date, and place of hearing or other official correspondence to the respondent's address. If a respondent fails to keep address information up to date, a hearing may be held in the respondent's absence, and the respondent may be ordered removed without being present. This is known as an "in absentia" order of removal.

Parties should note that notification to the Department of Homeland Security of a change in address does not constitute notification to the immigration court.

(1) Change of address or telephone number — Changes of address or telephone number must be in writing and *only* on the change of address form (Form EOIR-33/IC). Unless the respondent is detained, *no other means of notification are acceptable.* Changes in address or telephone numbers communicated through pleadings, motion papers, correspondence, telephone calls, applications for relief, or other means will *not* be recognized, and the address information on record will not be changed.

(2) Form EOIR-33/IC — The respondent should use only the most current version of the change of address form (Form EOIR-33/IC). The Form EOIR-33/IC is available at the immigration court and on the EOIR website. See also Chapter 11 (Forms) and Appendix D (Forms). Individuals in proceedings should observe the distinction between the immigration courts' Change of Address Form (Form EOIR-33/IC) and the Board of Immigration Appeals' Change of Address Form (Form EOIR-33/BIA). The immigration courts will not recognize changes in address or telephone numbers communicated on the Board of Immigration Appeal's Change of Address Form (Form EOIR-33/BIA), and the address information on record will not be changed. When submitted by an attorney or accredited representative, acting as a practitioner of record, the EOIR-33/IC must be submitted electronically through ECAS for all cases eligible for electronic filing and in paper in all other cases. When submitted by a pro se respondent or a practitioner of record other than an attorney or accredited representative, the Form EOIR-33/IC may be filed either in paper or electronically through the Respondent Access portal.

(3) Motions — A respondent should file a change of address form (Form EOIR-33/IC) when filing a motion to reopen, a motion to reconsider, or a motion to recalendar. This ensures that the immigration court has the respondent's most current address when it adjudicates the motion.

(d) Address Obligations of Detained Respondents — When a respondent is detained, the Department of Homeland Security (DHS) is obligated to report the location of the respondent's detention to the immigration court. DHS is also obligated to report when a respondent is moved between detention locations and when they are released. See 8 C.F.R. § 1003.19(g).

(1) While detained — As noted in (d), above, DHS is obligated to notify the immigration court when a respondent is moved between detention locations. See 8 C.F.R. § 1003.19(g).

(2) When released — The Department of Homeland Security is responsible for notifying the immigration court when a respondent is released from custody. 8 C.F.R. § 1003.19(g). Nonetheless, the respondent should file a change of address form (Form EOIR-33/IC) with the immigration court within 5 days of release from detention to ensure that immigration court records are current. See Chapter 2.2(c) (Address Obligations).

2.3   Attorneys

(a) Qualifications — Attorneys may represent individuals before the immigration court as the practitioner of record, or provide document assistance, only if they are members in good standing of the bar of the highest court of any state, possession, territory, or Commonwealth of the United States, or the District of Columbia, and are not under any order suspending, enjoining, restraining, disbarring, or otherwise restricting them in the practice of law. See 8 C.F.R. §§ 1001.1(f), 1292.1(a)(1). Any attorney appearing before the immigration court who is the subject of discipline in any jurisdiction must promptly notify EOIR's Office of the General Counsel. See Chapter 10.6 (Duty to Report). In addition, an attorney must be registered with EOIR in order to appear before the immigration court. See 8 C.F.R. § 1292.1(f), and Chapter 2.3(a)(1) (eRegistry), below.

(1) eRegistry — An attorney must register with EOIR through ECAS in order to appear before the immigration court and use ECAS. See 8 C.F.R. § 1292.1(f).

(A) Administrative suspension — If an attorney fails to register, they may be administratively suspended from practice before the immigration court. See 8 C.F.R. § 1292.1(f).

(B) Appearance by unregistered attorney — An immigration judge may, under extraordinary and rare circumstances, permit an unregistered attorney to appear at one hearing if the attorney files a Form EOIR-28, and provides, on the record, the following registration information: name; date of birth; business address(es); business telephone number(s); e-mail address; and bar admission information (including bar number if applicable) for all the jurisdictions in which the attorney is licensed to practice, including those in which they are inactive. See 8 C.F.R. § 1292.1(f). An unregistered attorney who is permitted to appear at one hearing in such circumstances must complete the electronic registration process without delay after that hearing.

(2) Address Obligations — All practitioners have an affirmative duty to keep the immigration court apprised of their current contact information, including address, email address, and telephone number. Changes in an attorney's address or contact information should be made by updating the registration information in EOIR's eRegistry to include the new address and contact information. See Chapter 2.1(b)(6) (Address Obligations of Practitioners).

(b) Appearances — Attorneys must complete the proper form to make an appearance before the immigration court. To perform the functions of and become the practitioner of record, an attorney must file a Form EOIR-28. See 8 C.F.R. § 1003.17(a); Chapter 2.1(b) (Entering an Appearance as the Practitioner of Record). Attorneys who have not filed a Form EOIR-28 to become the practitioner of record, and who provide assistance to pro se respondents with the drafting, completion, or filling in of blank spaces of a specific motion, brief, form, or other document or set of documents intended to be filed with the immigration court, must disclose such assistance by completing a Form EOIR-61, which must be filed along with the assisted document or set of documents. See 8 C.F.R. § 1003.17(b); Chapter 2.1(c) (Limited Appearance for Document Assistance).

(1) Completing Form EOIR-28 and Form EOIR-61 — If information is omitted from the Form EOIR-28 or Form EOIR-61, or they are not properly completed, the attorney's appearance may not be recognized, and any accompanying filing may be rejected. The following information must be completed by attorneys in completing a Form EOIR-28 or Form EOIR-61.

(A) Attorney information — The Form EOIR-28 and Form EOIR-61 must bear an attorney's current contact information, including address, email address, and telephone number, and the attorney's signature in compliance with the requirements of Chapter 3.3(b) (Signatures). When filing a paper Form EOIR-28 or Form EOIR-61, all information required on the form, including the date, should be typed or printed clearly. The EOIR ID number issued by EOIR through the eRegistry process must be provided on the Form EOIR-28 or Form EOIR-61.

(B) Bar information — When an attorney is a member of a state bar which has a state bar number or corresponding court number, the attorney must provide that number on the Form EOIR-28 or Form EOIR-61. If the attorney has been admitted to more than one state bar, *each and every* state bar to which the attorney has ever been admitted — including states in which the attorney is no longer an active member or has been suspended, expelled, or disbarred — must be listed and the state bar number, if any, provided.

(C) Disciplinary information — An attorney must not check the box regarding attorney bar membership and disciplinary action on the Form EOIR-28 and Form EOIR-61 if the attorney is subject to an order disbarring, suspending, or otherwise restricting the attorney in the practice of law. If the attorney is subject to discipline or otherwise restricted in the practice of law, then the attorney must provide additional information on the back of the form. (Attorneys may attach an explanatory supplement or other documentation to the form.) An attorney who fails to provide disciplinary information will not be recognized by the immigration court and may be subject to disciplinary action.

(c) Practitioner Misconduct — The Executive Office for Immigration Review has the authority to impose disciplinary sanctions upon practitioners who violate rules of professional conduct before the Board of Immigration Appeals, the immigration courts, and the Department of Homeland Security. See Chapter 10 (Discipline of Practitioners). Where a practitioner of record in a case has been suspended from practice before the immigration court and the respondent has not retained new counsel, the immigration court treats the respondent as unrepresented. In such a case, all mailings from the immigration court, including notices of hearing and orders, are mailed directly to the respondent. Any filing from a practitioner who has been suspended from practice before the immigration court is rejected. See Chapter 3.1(d) (Defective Filings).

2.4   Accredited Representatives and Recognized Organizations

(a) Generally — A fully accredited representative is a practitioner who is not an attorney and is approved by the Assistant Director for Policy or the Assistant Director's designee to make appearances before the Board, the immigration courts, and the Department of Homeland Security (DHS). A partially accredited representative is authorized to appear solely before DHS. An accredited representative must, among other requirements, have the character and fitness to represent respondents and be employed by, or be a volunteer for, a non-profit religious, charitable, social service, or similar organization that has been recognized by the Assistant Director for Policy or the Assistant Director's designee to represent respondents. 8 C.F.R. §§ 1292.1(a)(4), 1292.11(a), 1292.12(a)-(e). Accreditation of an individual is valid for a period of up to three years, and recognition of an organization is valid for a period of up to six years. 8 C.F.R. §§ 1292.11(f), 1292.12(d). Both may be renewed. 8 C.F.R. § 1292.16.

(b) Recognized Organizations — The Assistant Director for Policy or the Assistant Director's designee, in the exercise of discretion, may recognize an eligible organization to provide representation through accredited representatives. See 8 C.F.R. § 1292.11(a); Chapter 2.2(b) (List of Pro Bono Legal Service Providers). To be recognized by EOIR, an organization must affirmatively apply for that recognition. Such an organization must establish, among other requirements, that it: is a non-profit religious, charitable, social service, or similar organization; is a Federal tax-exempt organization; has at its disposal adequate knowledge, information, and experience in immigration law and procedure; and, if the organization charges fees, has a written policy for accommodating clients unable to pay fees for immigration legal services. The qualifications and procedures for organizations seeking recognition are set forth in the regulations. 8 C.F.R. §§ 1292.11, 1292.13. A recognized organization also has reporting, recordkeeping, and posting requirements. 8 C.F.R. § 1292.14. The R&A FAQs provide responses to the most common questions about recognition. Questions regarding recognition not addressed in the R&A FAQs may be directed to the Recognition and Accreditation Program in the EOIR Office of Policy. See Appendix A (Directory).

(c) Accredited Representatives —

(1) Qualifications — Recognized organizations, or organizations applying for recognition, may request accreditation of individuals who are employed by or volunteer for that organization. The Assistant Director for Policy or the Assistant Director's designee, in the exercise of discretion, may approve accreditation of an eligible individual. No individual may apply on their own behalf. Accreditation is not transferrable from one representative to another, and no individual retains accreditation upon separation from the recognized organization. The qualifications and procedures for individuals seeking accreditation are set forth in the regulations. 8 C.F.R. §§ 1292.12, 1292.13. In addition, a fully accredited representative must register with EOIR's eRegistry in order to practice before the immigration courts. See Chapter 2.4(c)(1)(A) (eRegistry). The R&A FAQs provide responses to the most common questions about accreditation.

(A) eRegistry — A fully accredited representative must register with EOIR's eRegistry in order to appear before the immigration court and use ECAS. See 8 C.F.R. § 1292.1(f).

- **Administrative suspension** — If a fully accredited representative fails to register, they may be administratively suspended from practice before the immigration court. See 8 C.F.R. § 1292.1(f).

- **Appearance by unregistered fully accredited representative** — An immigration judge may, under extraordinary and rare circumstances, permit an unregistered fully accredited representative to appear at one hearing if the accredited representative files a Form EOIR-28, and provides, on the record, the following registration information: name; date of birth; name of recognized organization; business address(es); business telephone number(s); and e-mail address. See 8 C.F.R. § 1292.1(f). An unregistered accredited representative who is permitted to appear at one hearing in such circumstances must complete the electronic registration process without delay after that hearing.

(B) Address Obligations — All practitioners have an affirmative duty to keep the immigration court apprised of their current contact information, including address, email address, and telephone number. Changes in an accredited representative's address or contact information should be made by updating the registration information in the EOIR eRegistry to include the new address and contact information. See Chapter 2.1(b)(6) (Address Obligations of Practitioners).

(2) Appearances — Fully accredited representatives must complete the proper form to make an appearance before the immigration court. To perform the functions of and become the practitioner of record, an accredited representative must file a Form EOIR-28. See 8 C.F.R. § 1003.17(a); Chapter 2.1(b) (Entering an Appearance as the Practitioner of Record). Fully accredited representatives who have not filed Form EOIR-28 to become the practitioner of record and who provide assistance to pro se respondents with the drafting, completion, or filling in of blank spaces of a specific motion, brief, form, or other document or set of documents intended to be filed with the immigration court must disclose such assistance by completing Form EOIR-61, which must be filed along with the assisted document or set of documents. See 8 C.F.R. § 1003.17(b); Chapter 2.1(c) (Limited Appearance for Document Assistance).

If information is omitted from Form EOIR-28 or Form EOIR-61, or they are not properly completed, the fully accredited representative's appearance may not be recognized, and any accompanying filing may be rejected.

(3) Immigration Specialists/Consultants — Accredited representatives should not be confused with non-lawyer immigration specialists/consultants, visa consultants, and "notarios." Chapter 2.7 (Immigration Specialists/Consultants). Accredited representatives must be expressly accredited by the Assistant Director for Policy or the Assistant Director's designee and must be employed by or volunteer for an organization specifically recognized by the Assistant Director for Policy or the Assistant Director's designee.

(4) Verification — To verify that an individual has been accredited by EOIR, please consult the Accredited Representatives List at https://www.justice.gov/eoir/recognition-accreditation-roster-reports.

(d) Accredited Representative and Recognized Organization Misconduct — Accredited representatives and recognized organizations must comply with certain standards of professional conduct. See 8 C.F.R. § 1003.101 et seq. The Executive Office for Immigration Review has the authority to impose disciplinary sanctions upon accredited representatives and recognized organizations who violate rules of professional conduct before the Board of Immigration Appeals, the immigration courts, and the Department of Homeland Security. See Chapter 10 (Discipline of Practitioners).

(e) Request to be Removed from List of Recognized Organizations or Accredited Representatives — A recognized organization or an accredited representative who no longer wishes to be on the Recognized Organizations and Accredited Representatives Roster must submit a written request to the Recognition and Accreditation Program. See Appendix A (Directory).

2.5   Law Students and Law Graduates

(a) Generally — Law students and law graduates (law school graduates who are not yet admitted to practice law) are practitioners who may appear before the immigration court if certain conditions are met and the appearance is approved by the immigration judge. Recognition by the immigration court is not automatic and must be requested in writing. See 8 C.F.R. § 1292.1(a)(2).

(b) Law Students —

(1) Qualifications — A law student participating in a legal aid program or clinic conducted by a law school or non-profit organization may appear in EOIR proceedings under the direct supervision of an EOIR-registered attorney or accredited representative. 8 C.F.R. § 1292.1(a)(2)(ii). The law student must not receive direct or indirect remuneration from the noncitizen they represent. 8 C.F.R. § 1292.1(a)(2)(ii).

(2) Appearances — The supervising attorney or accredited representative and the law student must complete the proper form, Form EOIR-28 or Form EOIR-61, and otherwise comply with the instructions below to make an appearance before the immigration court. If information is omitted from Form EOIR-28 or Form EOIR-61, they are not properly completed, or the instructions below are not followed, the supervising attorney or accredited representative's and the law student's appearances may not be recognized, and any accompanying filing may be rejected.

(A) Form EOIR-28 appearance — A law student is not permitted to register with the Executive Office for Immigration Review and, therefore, cannot electronically file documents, including a Form EOIR-28. See Chapter 2.1(b) (Entering an Appearance as the Practitioner of Record). Accordingly, the law student's supervising attorney or accredited representative must notify the immigration court of both individuals' appearances by filing two separate documents. The law student's supervising attorney or accredited representative must complete and submit a Form EOIR-28 as the practitioner of record in the proceeding. Together with that Form EOIR-28, the law student's supervising attorney or accredited representative must inform the immigration court of the law student's appearance by filing a "Notice of Representation by a Law Student" and a statement from the law student. The notice must include a copy of a Form EOIR-28 completed by the law student that indicates the law student's appearance is "[o]n behalf of [Attorney or Accredited Representative's Name] for the following hearing: [Date]." The statement from the law student must indicate that the student is appearing at the request of the noncitizen, that the student is participating in a legal aid program or clinic conducted by a law school or non-profit organization under the direct supervision of an EOIR-registered attorney or accredited representative, and that the student is appearing without direct or indirect remuneration from the noncitizen they represent. 8 C.F.R. § 1292.1(a)(2)(ii).

If the appearance is permitted by the immigration judge, the law student will not appear as the official practitioner of record for the proceeding. Instead, the law student's supervising attorney or accredited representative is the practitioner of record for the case and the person who submits all filings on behalf of the respondent whom the law student is helping to represent. 8 C.F.R. § 1292.1(a)(2)(v). The law student's supervisor is required to accompany the law student at any hearing and be prepared to proceed with the case at all times. 8 C.F.R. § 1292.1(a)(2)(iv). The immigration judge may permit the law student and supervising attorney or accredited representative to appear from separate physical locations.

(B) Form EOIR-61 limited appearance for document assistance — If the law student's supervising attorney or accredited representative and the law student have not filed Form EOIR-28s as discussed above, and the law student provides assistance to pro se respondents with the drafting, completion, or filling in of blank spaces of a specific motion, brief, form, or other document or set of documents intended to be filed with the immigration court, the supervising attorney or accredited representative and the law student must disclose such assistance by each completing a Form EOIR-61, which must be filed along with the assisted document or set of documents. See 8 C.F.R. § 1003.17(b); Chapter 2.1(c) (Limited Appearance for Document Assistance). Additionally, as above, the law student's Form EOIR-61 must be accompanied by a statement from the law student indicating that the student is appearing at the request of the noncitizen, that the student is participating in a legal aid program or clinic conducted by a law school or non-profit organization under the direct supervision of an EOIR-registered licensed attorney or accredited representative, and that the student is appearing without direct or indirect remuneration from the noncitizen.

(c) Law Graduates —

(1) Qualifications — A law graduate may appear in EOIR proceedings under the supervision of an EOIR-registered attorney or accredited representative. The law graduate must not receive direct or indirect remuneration from the noncitizen they represent. 8 C.F.R. § 1292.1(a)(2)(iii).

(2) Appearances — The supervising attorney or accredited representative and the law graduate must complete the proper form, Form EOIR-28 or Form EOIR-61, and otherwise comply with the instructions below to make an appearance before the immigration court. If information is omitted from Form EOIR-28 or Form EOIR-61, they are not properly completed, or the instructions below are not followed, the supervising attorney's or accredited representative's and the law graduate's appearances may not be recognized, and any accompanying filing may be rejected.

(A) Form EOIR-28 appearance — A law graduate is not permitted to register with the Executive Office for Immigration Review and, therefore, cannot electronically file documents, including a Form EOIR-28. See Chapter 2.1(b) (Entering an Appearance as the Practitioner of Record). Accordingly, the law student's supervising attorney or accredited representative must notify the immigration court of both individuals' appearances by filing two separate documents. The law graduate's supervising attorney or accredited representative must complete and submit a Form EOIR-28 as the practitioner of record in the proceeding. Together with that Form EOIR-28, the law graduate's supervising attorney or accredited representative must inform the immigration court of the law graduate's appearance by filing a "Notice of Representation by a Law Graduate" and a statement from the law graduate. The notice must include a copy of a Form EOIR-28 completed by the law graduate that indicates the law graduate's appearance is "[o]n behalf of [Attorney or Accredited Representative's Name] for the following hearing: [Date]." The statement from the law graduate must indicate that the graduate is appearing at the request of the noncitizen, that the graduate is under the supervision of an EOIR-registered attorney or accredited representative, and that the graduate is appearing without direct or indirect remuneration from the noncitizen they represent. 8 C.F.R. § 1292.1(a)(2)(iii).

The law graduate will not appear as the official practitioner of record for the proceeding. Instead, the law graduate's supervising attorney or accredited representative is the practitioner of record for the case and the person who submits all filings on behalf of the respondent whom the law graduate is helping to represent. 8 C.F.R. § 1292.1(a)(2)(v). The law graduate's supervisor is required to accompany the law graduate at any hearing and be prepared to proceed with the case at all times. 8 C.F.R. § 1292.1(a)(2)(v). The immigration judge may permit the law graduate and supervising attorney or accredited representative to appear from separate physical locations.

(B) Form EOIR-61 limited appearance for document assistance — If the law graduate's supervising attorney or accredited representative and the law graduate have not filed Form EOIR-28s as discussed above, and the law graduate provides assistance to pro se respondents with the drafting, completion, or filling in of blank spaces of a specific motion, brief, form, or other document or set of documents intended to be filed with the immigration court, the supervising attorney or accredited representative and the law graduate must disclose such assistance by completing Form EOIR-61s, which must be filed along with the assisted document or set of documents. See 8 C.F.R. § 1003.17(b); Chapter 2.1(c) (Limited Appearance for Document Assistance). Additionally, as above, the law graduate's Form EOIR-61 must be accompanied by a statement from the law graduate indicating that the graduate is appearing at the request of the noncitizen, that the graduate is under the supervision of an EOIR-registered licensed attorney or accredited representative, and that the graduate is appearing without direct or indirect remuneration from the noncitizen.

   (d) Practitioner Misconduct — Law students and law graduates must comply with standards of professional conduct. See 8 C.F.R. § 1003.101 et seq.

2.6 Paralegals

Paralegals are professionals who assist attorneys in the practice of law. They are not practitioners or licensed to practice law or to appear before the immigration court.

2.7 Immigration Specialists/Consultants

Immigration specialists/consultants—who include visa consultants and "notarios"—are *not* practitioners and are not authorized to practice law or to appear before the immigration court. They do not qualify either as accredited representatives or "reputable individuals" under the regulations. See Chapters 2.4 (Accredited Representatives and Recognized Organizations), 2.9(a) (Reputable Individuals). These individuals may be violating the law by practicing law without a license.

Anyone, including members of the public, may report instances of suspected misconduct by immigration specialists/consultants to the Executive Office for Immigration Review, Fraud and Abuse Prevention Program. See Additional Reference Materials, Chapter 8 (Fraud and Abuse Prevention Program).

2.8 Family Members

If a party is a child, then a parent or legal guardian may appear before the immigration court and represent the child, provided the parent or legal guardian clearly informs the immigration court of their relationship. If a party is an adult, a family member may represent the party *only* when the family member has been authorized by the immigration court to do so as a reputable individual. See Chapter 2.9(a) (Reputable Individuals).

2.9 Others

(a) Reputable Individuals — Reputable individuals are practitioners who may appear before the immigration court if certain conditions are met and the appearance is approved by the immigration judge. Recognition by the immigration court is not automatic and should be requested in writing. See 8 C.F.R. § 1292.1(a)(3).

(1) Qualifications — To qualify as a reputable individual and be permitted to appear, an individual must meet all of the following criteria, as found by an immigration judge in discretion:

- be a person of good moral character

- appear on an individual basis, at the request of the respondent

- receive no direct or indirect remuneration for their assistance of the respondent

- file a declaration that they are not being remunerated for their assistance of the respondent

- have a preexisting relationship with the respondent (e.g., relative, neighbor, clergy), except in those situations where representation would otherwise not be available

- be officially recognized by the immigration court.

Any individual who receives any sort of compensation or makes immigration appearances on a regular basis (such as a non-lawyer "immigration specialist," "visa consultant," or "notario") or holds themself out to the public as qualified to do so does not qualify as a "reputable individual" as defined in the regulations.

(2) Appearances — A reputable individual must complete the proper form, Form EOIR-28 or Form EOIR-61, and otherwise comply with the instructions below to make an appearance before the immigration court. If information is omitted from Form EOIR-28 or Form EOIR-61, they are not properly completed, or the instructions below are not followed, the reputable individual's appearance may not be recognized, and any accompanying filing may be rejected.

(A) Form EOIR-28 appearance — A reputable individual is not permitted to register with the Executive Office for Immigration Review and, therefore, cannot electronically file documents, including Form EOIR-28. See Chapter 2.1(b) (Entering an Appearance as the Practitioner of Record). Accordingly, to appear as the practitioner of record, a reputable individual must paper file a Form EOIR-28. Together with that Form EOIR-28, the reputable individual should include a statement demonstrating that the individual satisfies the qualification criteria in (a)(1) above.

(B) Form EOIR-61 limited appearance for document assistance — Because of the limited circumstances in which a reputable individual is permitted to appear, a reputable individual should seek to appear as the practitioner of record through the filing of a Form EOIR-28. However, If the reputable individual has not filed a Form EOIR-28 as discussed above, and the reputable individual provides assistance to pro se respondents with the drafting, completion, or filling in of blank spaces of a specific motion, brief, form, or other document or set of documents intended to be filed with the immigration court, the reputable individual must disclose such assistance by completing Form EOIR-61, which must be filed along with the assisted document or set of documents. See 8 C.F.R. § 1003.17(b); Chapter 2.1(c) (Limited Appearance for Document Assistance). Additionally, as above, the reputable individual's Form EOIR-61 must be accompanied by a statement from the reputable individual demonstrating that the individual satisfies the qualification criteria in section (a)(1) above.

(b) Fellow Inmates — The regulations do not provide for representation or appearances, including limited appearances for document assistance, by fellow inmates or other detained persons. Fellow inmates are not practitioners under the regulations.

(c) Accredited Officials of Foreign Governments — An accredited official of a foreign government to which the respondent owes an allegiance and who is in the

United States may appear before the immigration court as a practitioner if the appearance is in their official capacity and with the respondent's consent. See 8 C.F.R. § 1292.1(a)(5).

An accredited official must complete the proper form, Form EOIR-28 or Form EOIR-61, and otherwise comply with the instructions below to make an appearance before the immigration court. If information is omitted from Form EOIR-28 or Form EOIR-61, they are not properly completed, or the instructions below are not followed, the accredited official's appearance may not be recognized, and any accompanying filing may be rejected.

> **(1) Form EOIR-28 appearance** — An accredited official is not permitted to register with the Executive Office for Immigration Review and, therefore, cannot electronically file documents, including Form EOIR-28. See Chapter 2.1(b) (Entering an Appearance as the Practitioner of Record). Accordingly, to appear as the practitioner of record, an accredited official must paper file Form EOIR-28.

> **(2) Form EOIR-61 limited appearance for document assistance** — Because of the limited circumstances in which an accredited official is permitted to appear, an accredited official should seek to appear as the practitioner of record through the filing of Form EOIR-28. However, If the accredited official has not filed a Form EOIR-28 as discussed above and the accredited official provides assistance to pro se respondents with the drafting, completion, or filling in of blank spaces of a specific motion, brief, form, or other document or set of documents intended to be filed with the immigration court, the accredited official must disclose such assistance by completing Form EOIR-61, which must be filed along with the assisted document or set of documents. See 8 C.F.R. § 1003.17(b); Chapter 2.1(c) (Limited Appearance for Document Assistance). Additionally, the accredited official's Form EOIR-61 must be accompanied by evidence that the appearance is in an official capacity and that the respondent consented to the appearance.

(d) Former Employees of the Department of Justice — Former employees of the Department of Justice may be restricted in their ability to appear before the immigration court. See 8 C.F.R. § 1292.1(c).

(e) Foreign Student Advisors — Foreign student advisors, including "Designated School Officials," are not practitioners and are not authorized to appear before the immigration court, unless the advisor is an accredited representative. See Chapter 2.4 (Accredited Representatives and Recognized Organizations).

Chapter 3 Filing with the Immigration Court

3.1 Delivery and Receipt

(a) Filing — Documents are filed either with the immigration judge during a hearing or with the immigration court outside of a hearing. For documents filed outside of a hearing, the filing location is usually the same as the hearing location. However, for some hearing locations, documents are filed at a separate "administrative control court." See subsection (1), below, 8 C.F.R. §§ 1003.31, 1003.13.

> **(1) Administrative control courts** — "Administrative control courts" create and maintain the Records of Proceeding for the immigration courts within an assigned geographical area. 8 C.F.R. § 1003.11. A list of the administrative control courts along with their areas of assigned responsibility and other hearing locations is available to the public on the EOIR website.

> **(2) Shared administrative control** — In some instances, two or more immigration courts share administrative control of cases. Typically, these courts are located close to one another, and one of the courts is in a prison or other detention facility. Where courts share administrative control of cases, documents are filed at the hearing location. Cases are sometimes transferred between the courts without a motion to change venue. However, if a party wishes for a case to be transferred between the courts, a motion to change venue is required. See Chapter 5.10(c) (Motion to Change Venue). A list of courts with shared administrative control is available on the EOIR website.

> **(3) Receipt rule** — An application or document is not deemed "filed" until it is received by the immigration court. All submissions received by the immigration court are date-stamped on the date of receipt. Chapter 3.1(c) (Must be "Timely"). The immigration court does not observe the "mailbox rule." Accordingly, a document is not considered filed merely because it has been received by the U.S. Postal Service, commercial courier, detention facility, or other outside entity.

> **(4) Postage problems** — All required postage or shipping fees must be paid by the sender before an item will be accepted by the immigration court. When using a courier or similar service, the sender must properly complete the packing slip, including the label and billing information. The immigration court does not pay postage due or accept mailings without sufficient postage. Further, the immigration court does not accept items shipped by courier without correct label and billing information.

> **(5) Filings** — Filings sent through the U.S. Postal Service or by courier should be sent to the immigration court's street address. Hand-delivered filings should be brought to the immigration court's public window during that court's filing hours. Street addresses and hours of operation for the immigration courts are available on the EOIR website. Addresses are also available in Appendix A (Directory).

Given the importance of timely filing, parties are encouraged to use courier or overnight delivery services, whenever appropriate, to ensure timely filing. However, the failure of any service to deliver a filing in a timely manner does not excuse an untimely filing. See Chapter 3.1(c)(3) (Delays in delivery), below.

(6) Separate envelopes — Filings pertaining to unrelated matters should not be enclosed in the same envelope. Rather, filings pertaining to unrelated matters should be sent separately or in separate envelopes within a package.

(7) Faxes — The immigration court does not accept facsimiles ("faxes") unless the transmission has been specifically authorized by the immigration court staff or the immigration judge. Unauthorized transmissions are not made part of the record and are discarded without consideration of the document or notice to the sender.

(8) Electronic filing through ECAS — Electronic filing through ECAS is mandatory for attorneys and accredited representatives appearing as practitioners of record, as well as for DHS, in every case eligible for electronic filing. The immigration judge retains authority to accept paper filings at their sole discretion.

(b) Timing of Submissions — Filing deadlines depend on the stage of proceedings and whether the respondent is detained. Deadlines for filings submitted while proceedings are pending before the immigration court (for example, applications, motions, responses to motions, briefs, pre-trial statements, exhibits, and witness lists) are as specified in subsections (1), (2), and (3), below, unless otherwise specified by the immigration judge. Deadlines for filings submitted after proceedings before the immigration court have been completed are as specified in subsections (4) and (5), below.

Deadlines for filings submitted while proceedings are pending before the immigration court depend on whether the next hearing is a master calendar or an individual calendar hearing. In all cases, the immigration judge retains the authority to modify filing deadlines.

Untimely filings are treated as described in subsection (d)(2), below. Failure to timely respond to a motion may result in the motion being deemed unopposed. See Chapter 5.12 (Response to Motion). Immigration judges may deny a motion before the close of the response period without waiting for a response from the opposing party. See Chapter 5.12 (Response to Motion). "Day" is constructed as described in subsection (c), below.

(1) Master calendar hearings —

(A) Unrepresented, non-detained respondents — For master calendar hearings involving unrepresented, non-detained respondents, filings must be submitted at least fifteen (15) days in advance of the hearing if requesting a ruling at or prior to the hearing. Otherwise, filings may be made either in advance of the hearing or in open court during the hearing. When a filing is submitted at least fifteen days prior to a master calendar hearing, the response must be submitted within ten (10) days after the original filing with the immigration court. If a filing is submitted less than fifteen (15) days prior to a master calendar hearing, the response may be presented at the master calendar hearing, either orally or in writing.

(B) Represented, non-detained respondents — In proceedings in which the Form EOIR-28 is filed at least fifteen (15) days prior to a master calendar hearing, the hearing will be vacated. The immigration judge will issue a scheduling order that establishes the deadline by which the parties must submit written pleadings and any evidence related to the charge(s) of removability.

In proceedings in which the Form EOIR-28 is filed less than fifteen (15) days prior to the master calendar hearing, or at the master calendar hearing itself, the practitioner of record and the respondent must appear at the scheduled hearing. If needed, the immigration judge will issue a scheduling order at the master calendar hearing.

The parties generally will be given thirty (30) days from the date of the vacated hearing to submit written pleadings and any evidence related to the charge(s) of removability. Responses to the filings specified above should be filed within twenty (20) days after the original filing with the immigration court.

If the immigration judge finds that removability has been established, the court will issue a scheduling order establishing the deadline for the submission of any applications for relief or protection from removal and documents. The deadline will generally be sixty (60) days from the date of the order finding removability, unless otherwise ordered by the immigration judge. Failure to abide by the deadlines set by the immigration judge for the filing of applications may result in a finding that all applications for relief have been abandoned. A request for a master calendar hearing or an extension of the deadlines for filing should be made by written motion. See Chapter 3.1(c)(4) (Motions for extensions of filing deadlines), 3.1(c)(5) (Motions for master calendar hearing).

Where a master calendar hearing is held in a case involving a non-detained, represented respondent, filings must be submitted at least fifteen (15) days in advance of the hearing if requesting a ruling at or prior to the hearing. Otherwise, filings may be made either in advance of the hearing or in open court during the hearing. When a filing is submitted at least fifteen days prior to a master calendar hearing, the response must be submitted within ten (10) days after the original filing with the immigration court. If a filing is submitted less than fifteen (15) days prior to a master calendar hearing, the response may be presented at the master calendar hearing, either orally or in writing.

(C) Detained respondents — For master calendar hearings involving detained respondents, filing deadlines are as specified by the immigration court.

(2) Individual calendar hearings —

(A) Unrepresented, non-detained respondents — For individual calendar hearings involving unrepresented, non-detained respondents, filings must be submitted at least fifteen (15) days in advance of the hearing. This provision does not apply to exhibits or witnesses offered solely to rebut and/or impeach. Responses to filings that were submitted in advance of an individual calendar hearing must be filed within ten (10) days after the original filing with the immigration court. Objections to evidence may be made at any time, including at the hearing.

(B) Represented, non-detained respondents — For individual calendar hearings involving represented, non-detained respondents, amendments to applications for relief, additional supporting documents, updates to witness lists, and other such documents must be submitted at least fifteen (15) days in advance of the individual calendar hearing. This provision does not apply to exhibits of witnesses offered solely to rebut and/or impeach. Responses to filings must be filed within ten (10) days after the original filing with the immigration court. Objections to evidence may be made at any time, including at the hearing.

(C) Detained respondents — For individual calendar hearings involving detained respondents, filing deadlines are as specified by the immigration court.

(3) Asylum applications — Asylum applications in removal proceedings are categorized as either "defensive" or "affirmative." A defensive asylum application is filed with the immigration court by a noncitizen already in proceedings. An affirmative asylum application is filed with the Department of Homeland Security (DHS) Asylum Office by a noncitizen not in removal proceedings. If the DHS Asylum Office declines to grant an affirmative asylum application, removal proceedings may be initiated. In that case, the asylum application is referred to an immigration judge, who may grant or deny the application. See 8 C.F.R. § 1208.4.

A noncitizen filing an application for asylum should be mindful that the application must be filed within one year of arrival in the United States, unless certain exceptions apply. INA § 208(a)(2)(B), 8 C.F.R. § 1208.4(a)(2).

For information on asylum applications in streamlined removal proceedings, see Chapter 7.6 (Streamlined Removal Proceedings).

(A) Defensive applications — Defensive asylum applications are filed electronically, by mail, courier, in person at the court window, or in open court at a master calendar hearing.

(B) Affirmative applications — Affirmative asylum applications referred to an immigration court by the DHS Asylum Office are contained in the Record of Proceedings. Therefore, there is no need for the respondent to re-file the application with the immigration court. After being placed in immigration court proceedings, the respondent may amend their asylum application. For example, the respondent may submit amended pages of the application, as long as all changes are clearly reflected. Such amendments must be filed by the usual filing deadlines, provided in subsections (b)(1) and (b)(2), above. The amendment should be accompanied by a cover page with an appropriate caption, such as "AMENDMENT TO PREVIOUSLY FILED ASYLUM APPLICATION." See Appendix E (Cover Pages).

(4) Reopening and reconsideration — Deadlines for filing motions to reopen and motions to reconsider with the immigration court are governed by statute and regulation. See Chapter 5 (Motions before the Immigration Court). Responses to such motions are due within ten (10) days after the motion was received by the immigration court, unless otherwise specified by the immigration judge. See Chapter 5.7 (Motions to Reopen), Chapter 5.8 (Motions to Reconsider). See also Chapter 5.12 (Response to Motion).

(5) Appeals — Appeals must be received by the Board of Immigration Appeals no later than 30 calendar days after the immigration judge renders an oral decision or provides a written decision either by mail or electronic notification. See 8 C.F.R. § 1003.38, Chapter 6 (Appeals of Immigration Judge Decisions).

(6) Specific deadlines — The deadlines for specific types of filings are listed in Appendix C (Deadlines).

(c) Must be "Timely" — The immigration court places a date stamp on all documents it receives. Absent persuasive evidence to the contrary, the immigration court's date stamp is controlling in determining whether a filing is "timely." Because filings are date-stamped upon arrival at the immigration court, parties should file documents as far in advance of deadlines as possible.

(1) Construction of "day" — All filing deadlines are calculated in calendar days. Thus, unless otherwise indicated, all references to "days" in this Practice Manual refer to calendar days rather than business days.

(2) Computation of time — Parties should use the following guidelines to calculate deadlines.

(A) Deadlines on specific dates — A filing may be due by a specific date. For example, an immigration judge may require a party to file a brief by June 21, 2023. If such a deadline falls on a Saturday, Sunday, or legal holiday, the deadline is construed to fall on the next business day.

(B) Deadlines prior to hearings — A filing may be due a specific period of time *prior to* a hearing. For example, if a filing is due 15 days prior to a hearing, the day of the hearing counts as "day 0" and the day before the hearing counts as "day 1." Because deadlines are calculated using calendar days, Saturdays, Sundays, and legal holidays are counted. If, however, such a deadline falls on a Saturday, Sunday, or legal holiday, the deadline is construed to fall on the next business day.

(C) Deadlines following hearings — A filing may be due within a specific period of time *following* a hearing. For example, if a filing is due 15 days after a master calendar hearing, the day of the hearing counts as "day 0" and the day following the hearing counts as "day 1." Because deadlines are calculated using calendar days, Saturdays, Sundays, and legal holidays are counted. If, however, such a deadline falls on a Saturday, Sunday, or legal holiday, the deadline is construed to fall on the next business day.

(D) Deadlines following immigration judges' decisions — Pursuant to statute or regulation, a filing may be due within a specific period of time following an immigration judge's decision. For example, appeals, motions to reopen, and motions to reconsider must be filed within such deadlines. See 8 C.F.R. §§ 1003.38(b), 1003.23. In such cases, the day the immigration judge renders an oral decision or either mails or sends electronic notification of a written decision counts as "day 0." The following day counts as "day 1." Statutory and regulatory deadlines are calculated using calendar days. Therefore, Saturdays, Sundays, and legal holidays are counted. If, however, a statutory or regulatory deadline falls on a Saturday, Sunday, or legal holiday, the deadline is construed to fall on the next business day.

(E) Deadlines for responses — A response to a filing may be due within a specific period of time following the original filing. For example, if a response to a motion is due within 10 days after the motion was filed with the immigration court, the day the original filing is received by the immigration court counts as "day 0." The following day counts as "day 1." Because deadlines are calculated using calendar days, Saturdays, Sundays, and legal holidays are counted. If, however, such a deadline falls on a Saturday, Sunday, or legal holiday, the deadline is construed to fall on the next business day.

(3) Delays in delivery — Postal or delivery delays do not affect existing deadlines. Parties should anticipate all postal or delivery delays, whether a filing is made by first class mail, priority mail, or overnight or guaranteed delivery service. The immigration court does not excuse untimeliness due to postal or delivery delays, except in rare circumstances. See Chapter 3.1(a)(3) (Receipt rule), above.

(4) Motions for extensions of filing deadlines — Immigration judges have the authority to grant motions for extensions of filing deadlines that are not set by regulation. A deadline is only extended upon the *granting* of a motion for an extension. Therefore, the mere filing of a motion for an extension does not excuse a party's failure to meet a deadline. Unopposed motions for extensions are not automatically granted.

(A) Policy — Motions for extensions are not favored. In general, conscientious parties should be able to meet filing deadlines. In addition, every party has an ethical obligation to avoid delay.

(B) Deadline — A motion for an extension should be filed as early as possible and must be received by the original filing deadline.

(C) Contents — A motion for an extension should be filed with a cover page labeled "MOTION FOR EXTENSION" and comply with the requirements for filing. See Chapter 3 (Filing with the Immigration Court), Appendix E (Cover Pages). A motion for an extension should clearly state:

- when the filing is due

- the reason(s) for requesting an extension

- that the party has exercised due diligence to meet the current filing deadline

- that the party will meet a revised deadline

- if the parties have communicated, whether the other party consents to the extension

- a proposed revised deadline

(5) Motions for master calendar hearing — If a party believes that a master calendar hearing is necessary where a hearing has been vacated or none has been scheduled, the party must make a written motion for master calendar hearing. The motion should be filed with a cover page labeled "MOTION FOR MASTER CALENDAR HEARING" and comply with the requirements for filing. See Chapter 3 (Filing with the Immigration Court), Appendix E (Cover Pages). The motion should also clearly state:

- the date of the last master calendar hearing (if any)

- the reason(s) for requesting a master calendar hearing

- the best language for the respondent

- proposed dates and times (morning or afternoon) for the new hearing.

Examples of circumstances that may warrant a master calendar hearing include cases in which the respondent is an unaccompanied noncitizen child or exhibits indicia of mental incompetency.

(d) Defective Filings — Filings may be deemed defective due to improper filing, untimely filing, or both.

(1) Improper filings — If an application, motion, brief, exhibit, or other submission is not properly filed, it is rejected by the immigration court with an explanation for the rejection. Parties are expected to exercise due diligence. Parties wishing to correct the defect and refile after a rejection must do so promptly. See Chapters 3.1(b) (Timing of Submissions), 3.1(c) (Must be "Timely"). See also subsection (2), below. The term "rejected" means that the filing is returned to the filing party because it is defective and therefore will not be considered by the immigration judge. It is not an adjudication of the filing or a decision regarding its content. Examples of improper submissions include:

- if a fee is required, failure to submit a fee receipt or fee waiver request

- failure to include a proof of service upon the opposing party

- failure to comply with the language, signature, and format requirements

- illegibility of the filing

If a document is improperly filed but not rejected, the immigration judge retains the authority to take appropriate action.

(2) Untimely filings — The untimely submission of a filing may have serious consequences. The immigration judge retains the authority to determine how to treat an untimely filing. Accordingly, parties should be mindful of the requirements regarding timely filings. See Chapters 3.1(b) (Timing of Submissions), 3.1(c) (Must be "Timely").

Untimely filings, if otherwise properly filed, are not rejected by immigration court staff. However, parties should note that the consequences of untimely filing are sometimes as follows:

- if an application for relief is untimely, the respondent's interest in that relief is deemed waived or abandoned

- if a motion is untimely, it is denied

- if a brief or pre-trial statement is untimely, the issues in question are deemed waived or conceded

- if an exhibit is untimely, it is not entered into evidence or it is given less weight

- if a witness list is untimely, the witnesses on the list are barred from testifying

- if a response to a motion is untimely, the motion is deemed unopposed

(3) Motions to accept untimely filings — If a party wishes the immigration judge to consider a filing despite its untimeliness, the party must make an oral or written motion to accept the untimely filing. A motion to accept an untimely filing must explain the reasons for the late filing and show good cause for acceptance of the filing. In addition, parties are strongly encouraged to support the motion with documentary evidence, such as affidavits and declarations under the penalty of perjury. The immigration judge retains the authority to determine how to treat an untimely filing. EOIR will maintain an ECAS Outage Log that will note planned and unplanned ECAS system outages. Planned system outages will not impact filing deadlines since these can be proactively addressed by the parties. If EOIR determines that an unplanned outage has occurred, filing deadlines that occur on the last day for filing in a specific case will be extended until the first day of system availability that is not a Saturday, Sunday, or legal holiday.

(4) Natural or manmade disasters — Natural or manmade disasters may occur that create unavoidable filing delays. Parties wishing to file untimely documents after a disaster must comply with the requirements of subsection (3), above.

(e) Filing Receipts — The immigration court does not issue receipts for paper filings. Parties are encouraged, however, to obtain and retain corroborative documentation of delivery, such as mail delivery receipts or courier tracking information. As a precaution, parties should keep copies of all items sent to the immigration court. Parties who electronically file through ECAS will receive electronic notification upon successful upload and when the filing is accepted and added to the electronic record of proceeding.

(f) Conformed Copies — A time-and-date stamp is placed on each filing received by the immigration court. If the filing party desires a "conformed copy" (i.e., a copy of the filing bearing the immigration court's time-and-date stamp), the original must be accompanied by an accurate copy of the filing, prominently marked "CONFORMED COPY; RETURN TO SENDER." If the filing is voluminous, only a copy of the cover page and table of contents needs to be submitted for confirmation. The filing must also contain a self-addressed stamped envelope or comparable return delivery packaging. The immigration court does not return conformed copies without a prepaid return envelope or packaging. If a case has an eROP, ECAS users may download electronic copies of filings with watermarked time-and-date stamps through ECAS.

3.2   Service on the Opposing Party

(a) Service Requirements — The requirement to serve documents on the opposing party depends on whether both parties are participating in ECAS, as explained below.

(1) ECAS completes service — If all parties are using ECAS in a specific case, the parties do not need to separately serve any electronically filed documents on the opposing party. Rather, the ECAS system will automatically send service notifications to both parties that a new document has been filed. The parties must continue to include a certificate of service with their electronic filing, but simply note in the certificate that service was completed through ECAS.

For purposes of ECAS service, DHS is always considered to be participating in ECAS. Conversely, when DHS is electronically filing, EOIR will provide a notification to DHS users in the DHS Portal as to whether the opposing party is participating in ECAS or requires separate service.

(2) Separate service required — If one or more parties is not using ECAS in a specific case, or a specific document is not filed through ECAS, then the parties must complete service separately outside of the ECAS system.

If separate service is required, a party must:

- provide, or "serve," an identical copy on the opposing party (or, if the party is represented, the party's practitioner of record), and

- except for filings served during a hearing or jointly filed motions agreed upon by all parties, declare in writing that a copy has been served.

The written declaration is called a "Proof of Service," also referred to as a "Certificate of Service." See subsection (e), below, Appendix F (Cert. of Service).

(b) Whom to Serve — For a respondent in proceedings, the opposing party is the Department of Homeland Security (DHS). In most instances, a DHS Chief Counsel or a specific DHS Assistant Chief Counsel is the designated officer to receive service. Parties may contact the immigration court for the DHS address. The opposing party is never the immigration judge or immigration court.

(c) Method of Service — Service on the opposing party may be accomplished electronically, by hand-delivery, by U.S. Postal Service, or by commercial courier. Where service on the opposing party is accomplished by hand-delivery, service is complete when the filing is hand-delivered to a responsible person at the address of the individual being served.

Where service on the opposing party is accomplished by U.S. Postal Service or commercial courier, service is complete when the filing is deposited with the U.S. Postal Service or the commercial courier. Note that this rule differs from the rule for filings— filings with the immigration court are deemed complete when documents are received by the court, not when documents are mailed. See Chapter 3.1(a)(3) (Receipt rule).

(d) Timing of Service — The Proof of Service must bear the actual date of transmission and accurately reflect the means of transmission (e.g., electronic, hand delivery, regular mail, overnight mail, commercial courier, etc.). Service must be calculated to allow the other party sufficient opportunity to act upon or respond to served material.

(e) Proof of Service — A Proof of Service is required for all filings, except filings served on the opposing party during a hearing or jointly-filed motions agreed upon by all parties. See Appendix F (Cert. of Service). When documents are submitted as a package, the Proof of Service should be placed at the bottom of the package.

(1) Contents of Proof of Service — A Proof of Service must state:

- the name or title of the party served

- the precise and complete address of the party served

- the date of service

- the means of service (e.g., hand delivery, regular mail, overnight mail, commercial courier, etc.)

- the document or documents being served

A Proof of Service must contain the name and signature of the person serving the document. A Proof of Service may be signed by an individual designated by the filing party. In contrast, the document(s) being served must be signed by the individual who drafted or prepared the documents, whether DHS, an unrepresented respondent, a practitioner of record, or a practitioner who drafted, completed, or prepared the document(s) pursuant to a limited appearance for document assistance. See Chapter 3.3(b) (Signatures).

If service is being completed through ECAS, the Proof of Service should state, "This document was electronically filed through ECAS and both parties are participating in ECAS. Therefore, no separate service was completed."

(2) Certificates of Service on applications — Certain forms, such as the Application for Cancellation of Removal for Certain Permanent Residents (Form EOIR-42A), contain a Certificate of Service, which functions as a Proof of Service. Such a Certificate of Service only functions as a Proof of Service for the form on which it appears, not for any supporting documents filed with the form. If supporting documents are filed with an application containing a Certificate of Service, a separate Proof of Service for the entire submission must be included. If service is being completed through ECAS, the Proof of Service should state, "This document was electronically filed through ECAS and both parties are participating in ECAS. Therefore, no separate service was completed."

(f) Practitioner of Record and Service —

(1) Service on a practitioner of record — Service on a practitioner of record constitutes service on the person or entity represented. If a respondent is represented, the Department of Homeland Security must serve the respondent's practitioner of record but need not serve the respondent. See 8 C.F.R. § 1292.5(a), Chapter 2 (Appearances before the Immigration Court).

(2) Service by a represented respondent — Whenever a party is represented, documents are served by the practitioner of record (or the designee listed on the Proof of Service). See 8 C.F.R. § 1292.5(a), Chapter 2.1 (Representation and Appearances Generally).

(3) Service by an unrepresented respondent who received document assistance from a practitioner — A pro se respondent who received document assistance from a practitioner (or the designee listed on the Proof of Service) must serve the Department of Homeland Security with the completed Form EOIR-61 and document, or set of documents, on which they were provided assistance.

(g) Proof of Service and Notice of Appearance — All filings with the immigration court must include a Proof of Service that identifies the item being filed, unless served during a hearing. Thus, a completed Proof of Service on Form EOIR-28 or Form EOIR-61 does not constitute Proof of Service of documents accompanying the Form EOIR-28 or Form EOIR-61. See Chapter 3.2(f)(2) (Service by a represented respondent).

3.3   Documents

(a) Language and Certified Translations — All documents filed with the immigration court must be in the English language or accompanied by a certified English translation. See 8 C.F.R. §§ 1003.33, 1003.23(b)(1)(i). An affidavit or declaration in English by a person who does not understand English must include a certificate of interpretation stating that the affidavit or declaration has been read to the person in a language that the person understands and that they understood it before signing. The certificate must also state that the interpreter is competent to translate the language of the document, and that the interpretation was true and accurate to the best of the interpreter's abilities.

A certification of translation of a foreign-language document or declaration must be typed, signed by the translator, and attached to the foreign-language document. A certification must include a statement that the translator is competent to translate the language of the document and that the translation is true and accurate to the best of the translator's abilities. If the certification is used for multiple documents, the certification must specify the documents. The translator's address and telephone number must be included. See Appendix G (Cert. of Translation).

(b) Signatures — No forms, motions, briefs, or other submissions are properly filed without the signature, executed in ink or by digital or electronic means, of the individual who drafted or prepared the document(s), whether the Department of Homeland Security, an unrepresented respondent, a practitioner of record, or a practitioner who drafted, completed, or prepared the document(s) pursuant to a limited appearance for document assistance. Reproductions of signatures *are* acceptable when contained in a photocopy or fax of an original document as long as the original is available to the immigration court upon request. As circumstances require, all signatures are subject to authentication requirements.

For purposes of filing Form EOIR-28, the electronic acknowledgement and submission of an electronically filed Form EOIR-28 constitutes the signature of the respondent's practitioner of record. A Proof of Service also requires a signature but may be filed by someone designated by the filing party. See Chapter 3.2(e) (Proof of Service).

A signature represents a certification by the signer that: they have read the document; to the best of their knowledge, information, and belief formed after reasonable inquiry, the document is grounded in fact; the document is submitted in good faith; and the document has not been filed for any improper purpose. See 8 C.F.R. § 1003.102(j)(1). A signature represents the signer's authorization, attestation, and accountability. Every signature must be accompanied by the typed or printed name.

(1) Conformed and simulated signatures — For documents electronically filed through ECAS, a user who is logged in and electronically filing through ECAS may use a conformed signature wherever their personal signature is required. CONFORMED SIGNATURE EXAMPLE: /S/ John Doe. Otherwise, signature stamps are not acceptable on documents filed with the immigration court. These signatures do not convey the signer's personal authorization, attestation, and accountability for the filing. See also Chapters 3.1(a) (Filing), 3.3(d) (Originals and Reproductions).

(2) Law firms — Except as provided in Chapter 2.1(b)(8) (Appearances "on behalf of"), only a practitioner of record – not a law firm, law office, or other attorney – may sign a submission to the immigration court. See Chapters 2.1(b) (Entering an Appearance as the Practitioner of Record), 2.1(b)(4) (Multiple Practitioners), 2.1(b)(5) (Law Firms/Organizations).

(3) Accredited representatives — Accredited representatives must sign their own submissions.

(4) Paralegals and other staff — Paralegals and other staff are not authorized to practice before the immigration court and may not sign a submission to the immigration court. See Chapter 2.6 (Paralegals). However, a paralegal may sign a Proof of Service when authorized by the filing party. See Chapter 3.2(e) (Proof of Service).

(5) Other practitioners — Only those individuals who have been authorized by the immigration court to make appearances and have submitted a Form EOIR-28 or Form EOIR-61 may sign submissions to the immigration court. See Chapters 2.5 (Law Students and Law Graduates), 2.9 (Others).

(6) Family members — A family member may sign submissions on behalf of a party only under certain circumstances. See Chapter 2.8 (Family Members).

(c) Format — The immigration court prefers all filings and supporting documents to be typed but will accept handwritten filings that are legible. Illegible filings will be rejected or excluded from evidence. See Chapter 3.1(d) (Defective Filings). All filings must be signed by the individual who drafted or prepared the document(s) being filed, whether the Department of Homeland Security, an unrepresented respondent, a practitioner of record, or a practitioner who drafted, completed, or prepared the document(s) pursuant to a limited appearance for document assistance. See Chapter 3.3(b) (Signatures).

(1) Order of documents — Filings should be assembled as follows. All forms should be filled out completely. If a Form EOIR-28 or Form EOIR-61 is required, it should be submitted at the front of the package. See Chapter 2.1(b) (Entering an Appearance as the Practitioner of Record), 2.1(c) (Limited Appearance for Document Assistance). If a Form EOIR-28 has been filed electronically, a printed copy of the Form EOIR-28 is generally not required. See Chapter 2.1(b)(1) (How to File the Form EOIR-28).

(A) Applications for relief — An application package should comply with the instructions on the application. The application package should contain (in order):

- Form EOIR-28 or Form EOIR-61 (if required)

- Cover page

- If applicable, fee receipt (stapled to the application) or motion for a fee waiver

- Application

- Proposed exhibits (if any) with table of contents

- Proof of Service

See Chapters 2.1(b) (Entering an Appearance as the Practitioner of Record), 2.1(c) (Limited Appearance for Document Assistance), 3.2(e) (Proof of Service), 3.3(c)(6) (Cover page and caption), 3.3(e)(2) (Publications as evidence), 3.4 (Filing Fees).

(B) Proposed exhibits — If proposed exhibits are not included as part of an application package, the proposed exhibit package should contain (in order):

- Form EOIR-28 or Form EOIR-61 (if required)

- Cover page

- Table of contents

- Proposed exhibits

- Proof of Service

See Chapters 2.1(b) (Entering an Appearance as the Practitioner of Record), 2.1(c) (Limited Appearance for Document Assistance), Chapters 3.2(e) (Proof of Service), 3.3(c)(6) (Cover page and caption), 3.3(e)(2) (Publications as evidence), 3.4 (Filing Fees).

(C) Witness list — A witness list package should contain (in order):

- Form EOIR-28 or Form EOIR 61 (if required)

- Cover page

- Witness list (in compliance with the requirements of Chapter 3.3(g) (Witness Lists))

- Proof of Service

See Chapters 2.1(b) (Entering an Appearance as the Practitioner of Record), 2.1(c) (Limited Appearance for Document Assistance), 3.2(e) (Proof of Service), 3.3(c)(6) (Cover page and caption).

(D) Motions to reopen — A motion package for a motion to reopen should contain (in order):

- Form EOIR-28 or Form EOIR-61 (if required)

- Cover page

- If applicable, fee receipt (stapled to the motion or application) or motion for a fee waiver

- Motion to reopen

- A copy of the immigration judge's decision

- If applicable, a motion brief

- If applicable, a copy of the application for relief

- Supporting documentation (if any) with table of contents

- A change of address form (Form EOIR-33/IC) (recommended even if the respondent's address has not changed)

- A proposed order for the immigration judge's signature

- Proof of Service

See Chapters 2.1(b) (Entering an Appearance as the Practitioner of Record), 2.1(c) (Limited Appearance for Document Assistance), 2.2(c)(3) (Motions), 3.2(e) (Proof of Service), 3.3(c)(6) (Cover page and caption), 3.3(e)(2) (Publications as evidence), 3.4 (Filing Fees), 5 (Motions before the Immigration Court).

(E) Motions to reconsider — A motion package for a motion to reconsider should contain (in order):

- Form EOIR-28 or Form EOIR-61 (if required)

- Cover page

- If applicable, fee receipt (stapled to the motion or application) or motion for a fee waiver

- Motion to reconsider

- A copy of the immigration judge's decision

- If applicable, a motion brief

- If applicable, a copy of the application for relief

- Supporting documentation (if any) with table of contents

- A change of address form (Form EOIR-33/IC) (recommended even if the respondent's address has not changed)

- A proposed order for the immigration judge's signature

- Proof of Service

See Chapters 2.1(b) (Entering an Appearance as the Practitioner of Record), 2.1(c) (Limited Appearance for Document Assistance), 2.2(c)(3) (Motions), 3.2(e) (Proof of Service), 3.3(c)(6) (Cover page and caption), 3.3(e)(2) (Publications as evidence), 3.4 (Filing Fees), 5 (Motions before the Immigration Court).

(F) Other filings — Other filing packages, including pre-decision motions and briefs, should contain (in order):

- Form EOIR-28 or Form EOIR-61 (if required)

- Cover page

- If applicable, fee receipt (stapled to the filing) or motion for a fee waiver

- The filing

- Supporting documentation (if any) with table of contents

- If a motion, a proposed order for the immigration judge's signature

- Proof of service

See Chapters 2.1(b) (Entering an Appearance as the Practitioner of Record), 2.1(c) (Limited Appearance for Document Assistance), 3.2(e) (Proof of Service), 3.3(c)(6) (Cover page and caption), 3.3(e)(2) (Publications as evidence), 3.4 (Filing Fees).

(2) Number of copies — Except as provided in subsection (A) and (B), below, only the original of each application or other submission must be filed with the immigration court. For all filings, a copy may need to be served on the opposing party if required. See Chapter 3.2 (Service on the Opposing Party). Multiple copies of a filing (e.g., a brief, motion, proposed exhibit, or other supporting documentation) should not be filed unless otherwise instructed by the immigration judge.

(A) Defensive asylum applications — For defensive asylum applications, parties must submit to the immigration court the original application. See Chapter 3.1(b)(3)(A) (Defensive applications). In addition, a copy may need to be served on the opposing party if required. See Chapter 3.2 (Service on the Opposing Party).

(B) Consolidated cases — In consolidated cases, parties should submit a separate copy of each submission for placement in each individual Record of Proceedings. However, a "master exhibit" may be filed in the lead individual's file for exhibits and supporting documentation applicable to more than one individual, with the approval of the immigration judge.

(3) Pagination and table of contents — All documents, including briefs, motions, and exhibits, should always be paginated by consecutive numbers placed at the bottom center or bottom right-hand corner of each page.

Whenever proposed exhibits or supporting documents are submitted, the filing party should include a table of contents with page numbers identified. See Appendix N (Ex. Table of Contents).

Where a party is filing more than one application, the party is encouraged to submit a separate evidence package, with a separate table of contents, for each application.

(4) Tabs — For cases with paper ROPs, parties should use alphabetic tabs, commencing with the letter "A." The tabs should be affixed to the right side of the pages. In addition, parties should carefully follow the pagination and table of contents guidelines in subsection (3), above. If paper filing documents for a case with an eROP, parties are encouraged to use paper separators (i.e., a piece of paper with "Tab A" printed on it) instead of indexing tabs. This allows the immigration court to more easily scan the documents into the eROP.

(5) Paper size and document quality — All documents should be submitted on standard 8½" x 11" paper, in order to fit into the Record of Proceedings. See 8 C.F.R. § 1003.32(b). The use of paper of other sizes, including legal-size paper (8½" x 14"), is discouraged. If a document is smaller than 8½" x 11", the document should be affixed to an 8½" x 11" sheet of paper or enlarged to 8½" x 11". If a document is larger than 8½" x 11", the document should be reduced in size by photocopying or other appropriate means, as authorized by the immigration judge. This provision does not apply to documents whose size cannot be altered without altering their authenticity. All documents must be legible. Copies that are so poor in quality as to be illegible may be rejected or excluded from evidence. See Chapter 3.1(d) (Defective Filings).

Paper should be of standard stock white, opaque, and unglazed. Given its fragility and tendency to fade, photo-sensitive facsimile paper should never be used.

Ink should be dark, preferably black.

Briefs, motions, and supporting documentation should be single-sided.

(6) Cover page and caption — All filings should include a cover page. The cover page should include a caption and contain the following information:

- the name of the individual who drafted or prepared the documents being filed, whether the Department of Homeland Security, an unrepresented respondent, a practitioner of record, or a practitioner who drafted, completed, or prepared the document(s) pursuant to a limited appearance for document assistance

- the address of the above individual

- the title of the filing (such as "RESPONDENT's APPLICATION FOR CANCELLATION OF REMOVAL," "DHS WITNESS LIST," "RESPONDENT's MOTION TO REOPEN")

- the full name for each noncitizen covered by the filing (as it appears on the charging document)

- the A-number for each noncitizen covered by the filing (if a noncitizen has more than one A-number, all the A-numbers should appear on the cover page with a clear notation that the noncitizen has multiple A-numbers)

- the type of proceeding involved (such as removal, deportation, exclusion, or bond)

- the date and time of the hearing

See Appendix E (Cover Pages). If the filing involves special circumstances, that information should appear prominently on the cover page, preferably in the top right corner and highlighted (e.g., "DETAINED," "JOINT MOTION," "EMERGENCY MOTION").

(7) Fonts and spacing — Font and type size must be easily readable. "Times Roman 12 point" font is preferred. Double-spaced text and single-spaced footnotes are also preferred. Both proportionally spaced and monospaced fonts are acceptable.

(8) Binding — The immigration court and the Board of Immigration Appeals use a two-hole punch system to maintain paper files. All forms, motions, briefs, and other submissions should always be pre-punched with holes along the top (centered and 2 ¾" apart). Submissions may be stapled in the top left corner. If stapling is impracticable, the use of removable binder clips is encouraged. Submissions should neither be bound on the side nor commercially bound, as such items must be disassembled to fit into the record of proceedings and might be damaged in the process. The use of ACCO-type fasteners and paper clips is discouraged.

(9) Forms — Forms should be completed in full and must comply with certain requirements. See Chapter 11 (Forms). See also Appendix D (Forms).

(d) Originals and Reproductions —

(1) Briefs and motions — The original of a brief or motion must always be signed. See Chapter 3.3(b) (Signatures).

(2) Forms — The original of a form must always be signed. See Chapters 3.3(b) (Signatures), 11.3 (Submitting Completed Forms). In certain instances, forms must be signed in the presence of the immigration judge.

(3) Supporting documents — Photocopies of supporting documents, rather than the originals, should be filed with the immigration court and served on the Department of Homeland Security (DHS). Examples of supporting documents include identity documents, photographs, and newspaper articles.

If supporting documents are filed at a master calendar hearing, the respondent must make the originals available to DHS at the master calendar hearing for possible forensics examination at the Forensics Documents Laboratory. In addition, the respondent must bring the originals to all individual calendar hearings.

If supporting documents are filed after the master calendar hearing(s), the filing should note that originals are available for review. In addition, the respondent must bring the originals to all individual calendar hearings.

The immigration judge has discretion to retain original documents in the Record of Proceedings. The immigration judge notes on the record when original documents are turned over to DHS or the immigration court.

(4) Photographs — If a party wishes to submit a photograph, the party should follow the guidelines in subsection (3), above. In addition, prior to bringing the photograph to the immigration court, the party should print identifying information, including the party's name and A-number, on the back of the original photograph.

(e) Source Materials — Source materials should be provided to the immigration court and highlighted as follows.

(1) Source of law — When a party relies on a source of law in any filing (e.g., a brief, motion, or pre-trial statement) that is not readily available, that source of law should be reproduced and provided to the immigration court and the other party, along with the filing. Similarly, if a party relies on governmental memoranda, legal opinions, advisory opinions, communiques, or other ancillary legal authority or sources in any filing, copies of such items should be provided to the immigration court and the other party, along with the filing.

(2) Publications as evidence — When a party submits published material as evidence, that material must be clearly marked with identifying information, including the precise title, date, and page numbers. If the publication is difficult to locate, the submitting party should identify where the publication can be found and authenticated.

In all cases, the party should submit title pages containing identifying information for published material (e.g., author, year of publication). Where a title page is not available, identifying information should appear on the first page of the document. For example, when a newspaper article is submitted, the front page of the newspaper, including the name of the newspaper and date of publication, should be submitted where available, and the page on which the article appears should be identified. If the front page is not available, the name of the newspaper and the publication date should be identified on the first page of the submission.

Copies of State Department Country Reports on Human Rights Practices, as well as the State Department Annual Report on International Religious Freedom, must indicate the year of the particular report.

(3) Internet publications — When a party submits an internet publication as evidence, the party should follow the guidelines in subsection (2), above, as well as provide the complete internet address for the material.

(4) Highlighting — When a party submits secondary source material ("background documents"), that party should flag and emphasize the pertinent portions of that secondary source material. Any specific reference to a party should always be highlighted. Additionally, a party is encouraged to cite to specific pages or passages when referring to secondary source material within a brief or motion.

(f) Criminal Conviction Documents — Documents regarding criminal convictions must comport with the requirements of 8 C.F.R. § 1003.41. When submitting documents relating to a respondent's criminal arrests, prosecutions, or convictions, parties are encouraged to use a criminal history chart and attach all pertinent documentation, such as arrest and conviction records. The criminal history chart should contain the following information for each arrest:

- arrest date

- court docket number

- charges

- disposition

- immigration consequences, if any

The documentation should be paginated, with the corresponding pages indicated on the criminal history chart. For a sample, see Appendix M (Sample Criminal History Chart). Under "Immigration Consequences," parties should simply state their "bottom-line" position (for example: "not an aggravated felony"). Parties may supplement the criminal history chart with a prehearing brief. See Chapter 4.19 (Pre-Hearing Briefs).

(g) Witness Lists — A witness list should include the following information for each witness, except the respondent:

- the name of the witness

- if applicable, the A-number

- a written summary of the testimony

- the estimated length of the testimony

- the language in which the witness will testify

- a curriculum vitae or resume, if called as an expert

3.4   Filing Fees

(a) Where Paid — Fees for the filing of motions and applications for relief with the immigration court, when required, are paid to the Department of Homeland Security as set forth in 8 C.F.R. § 1103.7(a)(3). The immigration court does not collect fees. See 8 C.F.R. §§ 1003.24, 1103.7(a)(3).

(b) Filing Fees for Motions —

(1) When required — The following motions require a filing fee:

- a motion to reopen (except a motion that is based exclusively on a claim for asylum).

- a motion to reconsider (except a motion that is based on an underlying claim for asylum.

  For purposes of determining filing fee requirements, the term "asylum" here includes withholding of removal ("restriction on removal"), withholding of deportation, and claims under the Convention Against Torture and Other Cruel, Inhuman, or Degrading Treatment or Punishment. 8 C.F.R. §§ 1003.23(b)(1), 1003.24.

  Where a filing fee is required, the filing fee must be paid in advance to the Department of Homeland Security and the fee receipt must be submitted with the motion. If a filing party is unable to pay the fee, they should request that the fee be waived. See subsection (d), below.

  If the payer has paid any required fee but has not received the fee receipt from the Department of Homeland Security by the filing deadline set by the immigration judge, the payer must instead provide to the immigration court a copy of proof of the payment to the Department of Homeland Security with the filing. The payer must then submit a copy of the fee receipt by a new deadline set by the immigration judge. If the immigration judge does not set a deadline, the respondent must submit the fee receipt no later than 45 days after the date of filing of the application. 8 C.F.R. § 1103.7(a)(3).

(2) When not required — The following motions do not require a filing fee:

- a motion to reopen that is based exclusively on a claim for asylum

- a motion to reconsider that is based on an underlying claim for asylum

- a motion filed while proceedings are pending before the immigration court

- a motion requesting only a stay of removal, deportation, or exclusion

- a motion to recalendar

- any motion filed by the Department of Homeland Security

- a motion that is agreed upon by all parties and is jointly filed ("joint motion")

- a motion to reopen a removal order entered in absentia if the motion is filed under INA § 240(b)(5)(C)(ii)

- a motion to reopen a deportation order entered in absentia if the motion is filed under INA § 242B(c)(3)(B), as it existed prior to April 1, 1997

- a motion filed under law, regulation, or directive that specifically does not require a filing fee

8 C.F.R. §§ 1003.23(b)(1), 1003.24. For purposes of determining filing fee requirements, the term "asylum" here includes withholding of removal ("restriction on removal"), withholding of deportation, and claims under the Convention Against Torture and Other Cruel, Inhuman, or Degrading Treatment or Punishment.

(c) Application Fees —

(1) When required — When an application for relief that requires a fee is filed during the course of proceedings, the fee for that application must be paid in advance to the Department of Homeland Security (DHS). Instructions for paying application fees can be found in the DHS biometrics instructions, which are available from USCIS at https://www.uscis.gov/laws-and-policy/other-resources/immigration-benefits-in-eoir-removal-proceedings. A fee receipt must be submitted when the application is filed with the immigration court.

If a filing party is unable to pay the fee, the party should file a motion for a fee waiver. See subsection (d), below.

(2) When not required — When an application for relief that requires a fee is the underlying basis of a motion to reopen, the fee for the application need not be paid to the Department of Homeland Security (DHS) in advance of the motion to reopen. Rather, only the fee for the motion to reopen must be paid in advance. The fee receipt for the motion to reopen must be attached to that motion. See subsection (b)(1), above. If the motion to reopen is granted, the fee for the underlying application must then be paid to DHS and that fee receipt must be submitted to the immigration court. See Chapter 3.1(c) (Must be "Timely").

(d) When Waived — When a fee to file an application or motion is required, the immigration judge has the discretion to waive the fee upon a showing that the filing party is unable to pay the fee. However, the immigration judge will not grant a fee waiver where the application for relief is a Department of Homeland Security (DHS) form or DHS regulations prohibit the waiving of such fee. See 8 C.F.R. §§ 103.7(a)(1), 1103.7(c).

Fee waivers are not automatic but must be requested through the filing of a Fee Waiver Request (Form EOIR-26A). The Fee Waiver Request form must be filed along with the application or motion. The form requests information about monthly income and expenses and requires the applicant to declare, under penalty of perjury, that the applicant is unable to pay the fee due to personal economic hardship. If a fee waiver request does not establish the inability to pay the required fee, the requesting party will receive a rejection notice and the application or motion will be returned. However, the filer will be given 15-days to re-file the rejected application or motion with the fee or new fee waiver request, and any applicable filing deadline will be tolled during the 15-day cure period. 8 C.F.R. § 1003.24(d).

Fees are not reimbursed merely because the application or motion is granted.

In all cases, the immigration judge will issue a decision on a fee waiver request in writing or on the record.

(e) Amount of Payment —

(1) Motions to reopen or reconsider — When a filing fee is required, the fee for motions to reopen or reconsider is $145. The fee is paid to the Department of Homeland Security in advance. The fee receipt and motion are then filed with the immigration court.

(2) Applications for relief — Application fees are found in the application instructions and in the federal regulations. See 8 C.F.R. § 103.7. See also Chapter 11 (Forms), Appendix D (Forms).

(3) Background and security checks — The Department of Homeland Security (DHS) biometrics fee is found in the DHS biometrics instructions provided to respondents in the immigration court. 8 C.F.R. § 1003.47(d). The immigration judge cannot waive the DHS biometrics fee.

(f) Payments in Consolidated Proceedings —

(1) Motions to reopen and reconsider — Only one motion fee should be paid in a consolidated proceeding. For example, if several respondents in a consolidated proceeding file simultaneous motions to reopen, only one motion fee should be paid.

(2) Applications for relief — To determine the amount of the fee to be paid for applications filed in consolidated proceedings, the parties should follow the instructions on the application. In some cases, a fee is required for each application. For example, if each respondent in a consolidated proceeding wishes to apply for cancellation of removal, a fee is required for each application.

(g) Form of Payment — When a fee is required to file an application for relief or a motion to reopen or reconsider, the fee is paid to the Department of Homeland Security and the form of the payment is governed by federal regulations. See 8 C.F.R. § 103.7.

(h) Defective or Missing Payment — If a fee is required to file an application for relief or motion but a fee receipt is not submitted to the immigration court (for example, because the fee was not paid in advance to the Department of Homeland Security), the filing is defective and may be rejected or excluded from evidence. If a fee is not paid in the correct amount or is uncollectible, the filing is defective and may be rejected or excluded from evidence. See Chapter 3.1(d) (Defective Filings).

Chapter 4 Hearings before the Immigration Judges

4.1   Types of Proceedings

Immigration judges preside over courtroom proceedings in removal, deportation, exclusion, and other kinds of proceedings. See Chapter 1.4(a) (Jurisdiction). This chapter describes the procedures in removal proceedings.

Other kinds of proceedings, including streamlined removal proceedings under 8 C.F.R. § 1240.17, conducted by immigration judges are discussed in the following chapters:

Chapter 7	Other Proceedings before Immigration Judges
Chapter 9	Detention and Bond
Chapter 10	Discipline of Practitioners

Note: Prior to the Illegal Immigration Reform and Immigrant Responsibility Act of 1996 (IIRIRA), the two major types of courtroom proceedings conducted by immigration judges were deportation and exclusion proceedings. In 1996, the IIRIRA replaced deportation proceedings and exclusion proceedings with removal proceedings. The new removal provisions went into effect on April 1, 1997. See INA § 240, as amended by IIRIRA § 309(a). The regulations governing removal proceedings are found at 8 C.F.R. §§ 1003.12-1003.41, 1240.1-1240.26. For more information on deportation and exclusion proceedings, see Chapter 7 (Other Proceedings before Immigration Judges).

4.2   Commencement of Removal Proceedings

(a) Notice to Appear — Removal proceedings begin when the Department of Homeland Security files a Notice to Appear (Form I-862) with the immigration court after it is served on the respondent. See 8 C.F.R. §§ 1003.13, 1003.14. Individual DHS offices, including USCIS and ICE OPLA field offices, are not required to file a Notice to Appear with any particular immigration court, but EOIR maintains an administrative control court list as a guide for where DHS may file charging documents and which immigration courts generally have jurisdiction over particular DHS offices or detention locations. See Chapter 3.1(a)(1) (Administrative control courts). The Notice to Appear, or "NTA," is a written notice to the respondent which includes the following information:

- the nature of the proceedings

- the legal authority under which the proceedings are conducted

- the acts or conduct alleged to be in violation of the law

- the charge(s) against the respondent and the statutory provision(s) alleged to have been violated

- the opportunity to be represented by counsel at no expense to the government

- the consequences of failing to appear at scheduled hearings

- the requirement that the respondent immediately provide the Attorney General with a written record of an address and telephone number

The Notice to Appear replaces the Order to Show Cause (Form I-221), which was the charging document used to commence deportation proceedings, and the Notice to Applicant for Admission Detained for Hearing before an Immigration Judge (Form I-122), which was the charging document used to commence exclusion proceedings. See 8 C.F.R. § 1003.13.

(b) Failure to Prosecute — On occasion, an initial hearing is scheduled before the Department of Homeland Security (DHS) has been able to file a Notice to Appear with the immigration court. For example, DHS may serve a Notice to Appear, which contains a hearing date, on a respondent, but not file the Notice to Appear with the court until sometime later. Where DHS has not filed the Notice to Appear with the court by the time of the first hearing, this is known as a "failure to prosecute." If there is a failure to prosecute, the respondent and counsel may be excused until DHS files the Notice to Appear with the court, at which time a hearing is scheduled.

4.3 References to Parties and the Immigration Judge

The parties in removal proceedings are the noncitizen and the Department of Homeland Security (DHS). See Chapter 1.2(d) (Relationship to the Department of Homeland Security). To avoid confusion, the parties and the immigration judge should be referred to as follows:

- the noncitizen should be referred to as "the respondent"

- the Department of Homeland Security should be referred to as "the Department of Homeland Security" or "DHS"

- the attorney for the Department of Homeland Security should be referred to as "the Assistant Chief Counsel," "the DHS attorney," or "the government attorney"

- the respondent's practitioner of record, if an attorney, should be referred to as "the respondent's counsel" or "the respondent's attorney"

- the respondent's practitioner of record, if not an attorney, should be referred to as "the respondent's representative"

- the immigration judge should be referred to as "the immigration judge" and addressed as "Your Honor" or "Judge ___"

Care should be taken not to confuse the Department of Homeland Security with the immigration court or the immigration judge. See Chapter 1.4(e) (Department of Homeland Security).

4.4 Representation

(a) Appearances as Practitioner of Record — A respondent in removal proceedings may appear without representation ("pro se") or with representation from a practitioner of record. See Chapter 2 (Appearances before the Immigration Court). If a party wishes to be represented, they may be represented by an individual authorized to provide representation under federal regulations. See 8 C.F.R. § 1292.1. See also Chapter 2 (Appearances before the Immigration Court). Whenever a respondent is represented, the respondent should submit all filings, documents, and communications to the immigration court through their practitioner of record.

(b) Notice of Appearance — Practitioners before the immigration court must file a Notice of Entry of Appearance as Attorney or Representative Before the Immigration Court (Form EOIR-28) to perform the functions of and become the practitioner of record. See Chapter 2.1(b) (Entering an Appearance as the Practitioner of Record). If at any time after the commencement of proceedings there is a change in representation, the new practitioner must file a new Form EOIR-28, as well as complying with the other requirements for substitution of counsel, if applicable. See Chapters 2.1(b) (Entering an Appearance as the Practitioner of Record), 2.1(b)(2) (Scope of Representation), 2.1(b)(3)(B) (Substitution of counsel).

(c) Multiple Practitioners of Record — For guidance on the limited circumstances in which parties may be represented by more than one practitioner of record, see Chapters 2.1(b)(2) (Scope of Representation), 2.1(b)(4) (Multiple Practitioners).

(d) Withdrawal or Substitution — Withdrawal of counsel can be requested by oral or written motion. See Chapter 2.1(b)(3)(C) (Withdrawal of counsel). Substitution of counsel also can be requested by oral or written motion. See Chapter 2.1(b)(3)(B) (Substitution of counsel).

4.5 Hearing and Filing Location

There are more than 500 immigration judges in more than 60 immigration courts nationwide. The hearing location is identified on the Notice to Appear (Form I-862) or hearing notice. See Chapter 4.15(c) (Notification). Parties should note that documents are not necessarily filed at the location where the hearing is held. For information on hearing and filing locations, see Chapter 3.1(a) (Filing). If in doubt as to where to file documents, parties should contact the immigration court.

4.6 Form of the Proceedings

An immigration judge may conduct removal hearings:

- in person

- by video conference

- by telephone conference, except that evidentiary hearings on the merits may only be held by telephone if the respondent consents after being notified of the right to proceed in person or by video conference

See INA § 240(b)(2), 8 C.F.R. § 1003.25(c). See also Chapter 4.7 (Hearings by Video or Telephone Conference).

Upon the request of the respondent or the respondent's practitioner of record, the immigration judge has the authority to waive the appearance of the respondent and/or the respondent's practitioner of record at specific hearings in removal proceedings. See 8 C.F.R. § 1003.25(a). See also Chapter 4.15(m) (Waivers of Appearances).

4.7   Hearings by Video or Telephone Conference

(a) In General — Immigration judges are authorized by statute to hold hearings by video conference and telephone conference, except that evidentiary hearings on the merits may only be conducted by telephone conference if the respondent consents after being notified of the right to proceed in person or through video conference. See INA § 240(b)(2), 8 C.F.R. § 1003.25(c). See also Chapter 4.6 (Form of the Proceedings).

(b) Location of Parties — Where hearings are conducted by video or telephone conference, the immigration judge, the respondent, the DHS attorney, and the witnesses need not necessarily be present together in the same location.

(c) Procedure — Hearings held by video or telephone conference are conducted under the same rules as hearings held in person.

(d) Filing — For hearings conducted by video or telephone conference, documents are filed at the immigration court having administrative control over the Record of Proceedings. See Chapter 3.1(a) (Filing). The locations from which the parties participate may be different from the location of the immigration court where the documents are filed. If in doubt as to where to file documents, parties should contact the immigration court.

In hearings held by video or telephone conference, immigration judges often allow documents to be faxed between the parties and the immigration judge. Accordingly, all documents should be single-sided. Parties should not attach staples to documents that may need to be faxed during the hearing.

(e) More Information — Parties should contact the immigration court with any questions concerning an upcoming hearing by video or telephone conference.

4.8   Attendance

Immigration court hearings proceed promptly on the date and time that the hearing is scheduled. Any delay in the respondent's appearance at a master calendar or individual calendar hearing may result in the hearing being held "in absentia" (in the respondent's absence). See 8 C.F.R. § 1003.26. See also Chapters 4.15 (Master Calendar Hearing), 4.16 (Individual Calendar Hearing), 4.17 (In Absentia Hearing).

Any delay in the appearance of either the Department of Homeland Security or the practitioner of record without satisfactory notice and explanation to the immigration court may, in the discretion of the immigration judge, result in the hearing being held in their absence.

Respondents, practitioners, and witnesses should be mindful that they may encounter delays in going through the mandatory security screening at the immigration court and should plan accordingly. See Chapter 4.14 (Access to Court). Regardless of such delays, all individuals must pass through the security screening and be present in the courtroom at the time the hearing is scheduled.

For hearings at detention facilities, parties should be mindful of any additional security restrictions at the facility. See Chapter 4.14 (Access to Court). Individuals attending such a hearing must always be present at the time the hearing is scheduled, regardless of any such additional security restrictions.

4.9   Public Access

(a) General Public

(1) Hearings — Hearings in removal proceedings are generally open to the public. However, special rules apply in the following instances:

- Evidentiary hearings involving an application for asylum or withholding of removal ("restriction on removal"), or a claim brought under the Convention Against Torture and Other Cruel, Inhuman, or Degrading Treatment or Punishment, are open to the public unless the respondent expressly requests that the hearing be closed. In cases involving these applications or claims, the immigration judge inquires whether the respondent requests such closure.

- Hearings involving an abused noncitizen child are closed to the public. Hearings involving an abused noncitizen spouse are closed to the public unless the abused spouse agrees that the hearing and the Record of Proceedings will be open to the public.

- Proceedings are closed to the public if information may be considered which is subject to a protective order and was filed under seal.

See 8 C.F.R. §§ 1003.27, 1003.31(d), 1003.46, 1208.6, 1240.10(b), 1240.11(c)(3)(i). Only parties, the practitioner(s) of record, employees of the Department of Justice, and persons authorized by the immigration judge may attend a closed hearing.

(2) Immigration judges authorized to close hearings — The immigration judge may limit attendance or close a hearing to protect parties, witnesses, or the public interest, even if the hearing would normally be open to the public. See 8 C.F.R. § 1003.27(b).

(3) Motions to close hearing — For hearings not subject to the special rules in subsection (1), above, parties may make an oral or written motion asking that the immigration judge close the hearing. See 8 C.F.R. § 1003.27(b). The motion should set forth in detail the reason(s) for requesting that the hearing be closed. If in writing, the motion should include a cover page labeled "MOTION FOR CLOSED HEARING" and comply with the deadlines and requirements for filing. See Chapter 3 (Filing with the Immigration Court), Appendix E (Cover Pages).

(b) News Media — Representatives of the news media may attend hearings that are open to the public. The news media are subject to the general prohibition on electronic devices in the courtroom. See Chapter 4.13 (Electronic Devices). The news media are strongly encouraged to notify the Communications and Legislative Affairs

Division and the court administrator before attending a hearing. See Appendix A (Directory).

4.10 Record

(a) Hearings Recorded — Immigration hearings are recorded electronically by the immigration judge. See 8 C.F.R. § 1240.9. Parties may listen to recordings of hearings by prior arrangement with immigration court staff. See Chapters 1.5(c) (Records), 12.2 (Requests).

The entire hearing is recorded except for those occasions when the immigration judge authorizes an off-the-record discussion. On those occasions, the results of the off-the-record discussion are summarized by the immigration judge on the record. The immigration judge asks the parties if the summary is true and complete, and the parties are given the opportunity to add to or amend the summary, as appropriate. Parties should request such a summary from the immigration judge, if the immigration judge does not offer one.

(b) Transcriptions — If an immigration judge's decision is appealed to the Board of Immigration Appeals, the hearing is transcribed in appropriate cases and a transcript is sent to both parties. For information on transcriptions, parties should consult the Board of Immigration Appeals Practice Manual.

(c) Record of Proceedings — The official file containing the documents relating to a respondent's case is the Record of Proceedings, which is created by the immigration court. The contents of the Record of Proceedings vary from case to case. However, at the conclusion of immigration court proceedings, the Record of Proceedings generally contains the Notice to Appear (Form I-862), hearing notice(s), the practitioner of record's Form EOIR-28 (if any), any change of address form(s) (Change of Address/Contact Information Form, Form EOIR-33), application(s) for relief, exhibits, motion(s), brief(s), hearing tapes (if any), and all written orders and decisions of the immigration judge.

4.11 Interpreters

Interpreters are provided at government expense to individuals whose command of the English language is inadequate to fully understand and participate in removal proceedings. In general, the immigration court endeavors to accommodate the language needs of all respondents and witnesses. The immigration court will arrange for an interpreter both during the individual calendar hearing and, if necessary, the master calendar hearing. See 8 C.F.R. § 1003.22, Chapter 4.15(o) (Other Requests).

The immigration court uses staff interpreters employed by the immigration court, contract interpreters, and telephonic interpretation services. Staff interpreters take an oath to interpret and translate accurately at the time they are employed by the Department of Justice. Contract interpreters take an oath to interpret and translate accurately in court. See 8 C.F.R. § 1003.22.

4.12   Courtroom Decorum

(a) Addressing the Immigration Judge — The immigration judge should be addressed as either "Your Honor" or "Judge __." See Chapter 4.3 (References to Parties and the Immigration Judge). The parties should stand when the immigration judge enters and exits the courtroom.

(b) Attire — All persons appearing in the immigration court should respect the decorum of the court. Practitioners should appear in business attire. All others should appear in proper attire.

(c) Conduct — All persons appearing in the immigration court should respect the dignity of the proceedings. No food or drink may be brought into the courtroom, except as specifically permitted by the immigration judge. Disruptive behavior in the courtroom or waiting area is not tolerated.

(1) Communication between the parties — Except for questions directed at witnesses, parties should not converse, discuss, or debate with each other or another person during a hearing. All oral argument and statements made during a hearing must be directed to the immigration judge. Discussions that are not relevant to the proceedings should be conducted outside the courtroom.

(2) Practitioners — Practitioners should observe the professional conduct rules and regulations of their licensing authorities. Practitioners should present a professional demeanor at all times.

(3) Minors — Children in removal proceedings must attend all scheduled hearings unless their appearance has been waived by the immigration judge. Unless participating in a hearing, children should not be brought to the immigration court. If a child disrupts a hearing, the hearing may be postponed with the delay attributed to the party who brought the child. Children are not allowed to stay in the waiting area without supervision.

For immigration courts in Department of Homeland Security detention facilities or federal, state, or local correctional facilities, the facility's rules regarding the admission of children, practitioners, witnesses, and family members will apply in addition to this subsection. See Chapter 4.14 (Access to Court).

4.13   Electronic Devices

(a) Recording Devices — Removal proceedings may only be recorded with the equipment used by the immigration judge. No device of any kind, including cameras, video recorders, and cassette recorders, may be used by any person other than the immigration judge to record any part of a hearing. See 8 C.F.R. § 1003.28.

(b) Possession of Electronic Devices during Hearings — Subject to subsection (c), below, all persons, including parties and members of the press, may keep in their possession laptop computers, cellular telephones, electronic calendars, and other electronic devices commonly used to conduct business activities, including electronic devices which have collateral recording capability. All electronic devices must be turned off in courtrooms and during hearings, unless otherwise authorized under subsection (c) below. Outside of courtrooms and hearings, electronic devices may be used in non-recording mode, but they must be made silent, and usage must be limited and non-disruptive. No device may be used by any person other than the immigration judge to record any part of a hearing. See subsection (a), above. For further discussion on the use of electronic devices, see EOIR Policy Memorandum 19-10, *EOIR Security Directive: Policy for Public Use of Electronic Devices in EOIR Space* (Mar. 20, 2019).

(c) Use of Electronic Devices during Hearings — In any hearing before an immigration judge, only practitioners of record and attorneys from DHS representing the government may use laptop computers, electronic calendars, and other electronic devices commonly used to conduct business activities, provided they are used to conduct immediately relevant court and business-related activities. Such devices may only be used in silent/vibrate mode. The use of such devices must not disrupt the hearing, and the immigration judge has the discretion to prohibit the continued use of any electronic devices that pose a disruption to ongoing proceedings. Cellular telephones and other electronic devices must be turned off when not in use to conduct business activities in the courtroom. No device may be used by any person other than the immigration judge to record any part of a hearing. See subsection (a), above. For further discussion on the use of electronic devices, see EOIR Policy Memorandum 19-10, *EOIR Security Directive: Policy for Public Use of Electronic Devices in EOIR Space* (Mar. 20, 2019).

(d) Courtrooms Administered under Agreement — In any immigration court or detention facility administered under agreement between the Executive Office for Immigration Review and federal, state, or local authorities, the facility's rules regarding the possession and use of electronic devices shall apply in addition to subsections (a) through (c), above. In some facilities, individuals, including practitioners, are not allowed to bring cellular telephones, laptop computers, and other electronic devices into the facility.

4.14 Access to Court

(a) Security Screening

(1) All immigration courts — All immigration courts require individuals attending a hearing to pass through security screening prior to entering the court. All individuals attending a hearing should be mindful that they may encounter delays in passing through the security screening.

(2) Detention facilities — For hearings held in Department of Homeland Security detention facilities or federal, state, or local correctional facilities, compliance with additional security restrictions may be required. For example, individuals may be required to obtain advance clearance to enter the facility. In addition, cellular telephones, laptop computers, and other electronic devices are not allowed at some of these facilities. All persons attending a hearing at such a facility should be aware of the security restrictions in advance. Such individuals should contact the immigration court or the detention facility in advance if they have specific questions related to these restrictions.

(3) Timeliness required — Respondents, practitioners, and witnesses must always be present in the courtroom at the time the hearing is scheduled. This applies regardless of any delays encountered in complying with the mandatory security screening and, if the hearing is held at a detention facility, with any additional security restrictions. See Chapter 4.8 (Attendance).

(b) No Access to Administrative Offices — Access to each immigration court's administrative offices is limited to immigration court staff and other authorized personnel. Parties appearing in immigration court or conducting business with the immigration court are not allowed access to telephones, photocopying machines, or other equipment within the immigration court's administrative offices.

4.15 Master Calendar Hearing

(a) Generally — Master calendar hearings are held for pleadings, scheduling, and other similar matters. See subsection (e), below.

(b) Request for a Prompt Hearing — To allow the respondent an opportunity to obtain representation from a practitioner and to prepare to respond, at least ten days must elapse between service of the Notice to Appear (Form I-862) on the respondent and the initial master calendar hearing. The respondent may waive this ten-day requirement by signing the "Request for Prompt Hearing" contained in the Notice to Appear. The respondent may then be scheduled for a master calendar hearing within the ten-day period. See INA § 239(b)(1).

(c) Notification — The Notice to Appear (Form I-862) served on the respondent may contain notice of the date, time, and location of the initial master calendar hearing. If so, the respondent must appear at that date, time, and location. If the Notice to Appear does not contain notice of the date, time, and location of the initial master calendar hearing, the respondent will be mailed a notice of hearing containing this information. If there are any changes to the date, time, or location of a master calendar hearing, the respondent will be notified by mail at the address on record with the immigration court. See Chapter 2.2(c) (Address Obligations).

(d) Arrival — Parties should arrive at the immigration court prior to the time set for the master calendar hearing. Practitioners of record should check in with the immigration court staff and sign in, if a sign-in sheet is available. Parties should be mindful that they may encounter delays in passing through mandatory security screening prior to entering the court. See Chapters 4.8 (Attendance), 4.14 (Access to Court).

(e) Scope of the Master Calendar Hearing — As a general matter, the purpose of the master calendar hearing is to:

- advise the respondent of the right to a practitioner at no expense to the government

- advise the respondent of the availability of pro bono legal service providers and provide the respondent with a list of such providers in the area where the hearing is being conducted

- advise the respondent of the right to present evidence

- advise the respondent of the right to examine and object to evidence and to cross-examine any witnesses presented by the Department of Homeland Security

- explain the charges and factual allegations contained in the Notice to Appear (Form I-862) to the respondent in non-technical language

- take pleadings

- identify and narrow the factual and legal issues

- set deadlines for filing applications for relief, briefs, motions, pre-hearing statements, exhibits, witness lists, and other documents

- provide certain warnings related to background and security investigations

- schedule hearings to adjudicate contested matters and applications for relief

- advise the respondent of the consequences of failing to appear at subsequent hearings

- advise the respondent of the right to appeal to the Board of Immigration Appeals

See INA §§ 240(b)(4), 240(b)(5), 8 C.F.R. §§ 1240.10, 1240.15.

(f) Opening of a Master Calendar Hearing — The immigration judge turns on the recording equipment at the beginning of the master calendar hearing. The hearing is recorded except for off-the-record discussions. See Chapter 4.10 (Record). On the record, the immigration judge identifies the type of proceeding being conducted (e.g., a removal proceeding); the respondent's name and A-number; the date, time, and place of the proceeding; and the presence of the parties. The immigration judge also verifies the respondent's name, address, and telephone number. If the respondent's address or telephone number have changed, the respondent must submit a change of address form (Change of Address/Contact Information Form, Form EOIR-33), Form EOIR-33/IC).

If necessary, an interpreter is provided to a respondent whose command of the English language is inadequate to fully understand and participate in the hearing. See Chapter 4.11 (Interpreters), subsection (o), below. If necessary, the respondent is placed under oath.

(g) Pro Se Respondent — If the respondent is unrepresented ("pro se") at a master calendar hearing, the immigration judge advises the respondent of their hearing rights and obligations, including the right to be represented by a practitioner at no expense to the government. In addition, the immigration judge ensures that the respondent has received a list of pro bono legal service providers in the area where the hearing is being held. The respondent may waive the right to be represented and choose to proceed pro se. Alternatively, the respondent may request that the immigration judge continue the proceedings to another master calendar hearing to give the respondent an opportunity to obtain representation.

If the proceedings are continued but the respondent is not represented at the next master calendar hearing, the respondent will be expected to explain their efforts to obtain representation. The immigration judge may decide to proceed with pleadings at that hearing or to continue the matter again to allow the respondent to obtain representation. If the immigration judge decides to proceed with pleadings, they advise the respondent of any relief for which the respondent appears to be eligible. Even if the respondent is required to enter pleadings without representation, the respondent still has the right to obtain representation before the next hearing. See Chapter 4.4 (Representation).

(h) Entry of Appearance as Practitioner of Record — If a respondent is represented, the practitioner of record should file any routinely submitted documents at the beginning of the master calendar hearing. The practitioner of record must also serve such documents on the opposing party if required. See Chapter 3.2 (Service on the Opposing Party). Routinely submitted documents include the Notice of Appearance (Form EOIR-28) and the change of address form (Form EOIR-33/IC). See Chapters 2.1(b) (Entering an Appearance as the Practitioner of Record), 2.2(c) (Address Obligations), 2.1(b)(6)(B) (Address obligations of represented respondents).

(i) Pleadings — At the master calendar hearing, the parties should be prepared to plead as follows.

(1) Respondent — The respondent should be prepared:

- to concede or deny service of the Notice to Appear (Form I-862)

- to request or waive a formal reading of the Notice to Appear (Form I-862)

- to request or waive an explanation of the respondent's rights and obligations in removal proceedings

- to admit or deny the charges and factual allegations in the Notice to Appear (Form I-862)

- to designate or decline to designate a country of removal

- to state what applications(s) for relief from removal, if any, the respondent intends to file

- to identify and narrow the legal and factual issues

- to estimate (in hours) the amount of time needed to present the case at the individual calendar hearing

- to request a date on which to file the application(s) for relief, if any, with the immigration court

- to request an interpreter for the respondent and witnesses, if needed

A sample oral pleading is included in Appendix L (Sample Oral Pleading). To make the master calendar hearing process more expeditious and efficient, practitioners of record are strongly encouraged to use this oral pleading format.

(2) Department of Homeland Security — The DHS attorney should be prepared:

- to state DHS's position on all legal and factual issues, including eligibility for relief

- to designate a country of removal

- to file with the immigration court and serve on the opposing party all documents that support the charges and factual allegations in the Notice to Appear (Form I-862)

- to serve on the respondent the DHS biometrics instructions, if appropriate

(j) Written Pleadings — In lieu of oral pleadings, the immigration judge may permit represented parties to file written pleadings, if the party concedes proper service of the Notice to Appear (Form I-862). See Appendix K (Sample Written Pleading). The written pleadings must be signed by the respondent and the respondent's practitioner of record.

The written pleading should contain the following:

- a concession that the Notice to Appear (Form I-862) was properly served on the respondent

- a representation that the hearing rights set forth in 8 C.F.R. § 1240.10 have been explained to the respondent

- a representation that the consequences of failing to appear in immigration court have been explained to the respondent

- an admission or denial of the factual allegations in the Notice to Appear (Form I-862)

- a concession or denial of the charge(s) in the Notice to Appear (Form I-862)

- a designation of, or refusal to designate, a country of removal

- an identification of the application(s) for relief from removal, if any, the respondent intends to file

- a representation that any application(s) for relief will be filed in accordance with the deadlines directed by the immigration judge, or, if the immigration judge has not directed a deadline, the deadlines contained in the Immigration Court Practice Manual

- an estimate of the number of hours required for the individual calendar hearing

- a request for an interpreter, if needed, that follows the guidelines in subsection (o), below

- if background and security investigations are required, a representation that:

- the respondent has been provided Department of Homeland Security (DHS) biometrics instructions

- the DHS biometrics instructions have been explained to the respondent

- the respondent will timely comply with the DHS biometrics instructions prior to the individual calendar hearing

- the consequences of failing to comply with the DHS biometrics instructions have been explained to the respondent

- a representation by the respondent that they:

- understand the rights set forth in 8 C.F.R. § 1240.10 and waive a further explanation of those rights by the immigration judge

- if applying for asylum, understand the consequences under INA § 208(d)(6) of knowingly filing or making a frivolous asylum application

- understand the consequences of failing to appear in immigration court or for a scheduled departure

- understand the consequences of failing to comply with the DHS biometrics instructions

- knowingly and voluntarily waive the oral notice required by INA § 240(b)(7) regarding limitations on discretionary relief following an in absentia removal order, or authorize their practitioner of record to waive such notice

- understand the requirement in 8 C.F.R. § 1003.15(d) to file a change of address form (Change of Address/Contact Information Form, Form EOIR-33) with the immigration court within five (5) days of moving or changing a telephone number

Additional matters may be included in the written pleading when appropriate. For example, the party may need to provide more specific information in connection with a request for an interpreter. See subsection (o), below.

(k) Background Checks and Security Investigations — For certain applications for relief from removal, the Department of Homeland Security (DHS) is required to complete background and security investigations. See 8 C.F.R. § 1003.47.

For non-covered relief, such investigations are not required but may warrant a discretionary grant of a continuance for DHS to complete the investigations. See 8 C.F.R § 1003.47(j)-(k). Questions regarding background checks and security investigations should be addressed to DHS.

(1) **Non-detained cases** — If a non-detained respondent seeks relief requiring background and security investigations, the DHS attorney provides the respondent with the DHS biometrics instructions. The respondent is expected to promptly comply with the DHS biometrics instructions by the deadlines set by the immigration judge. Failure to timely comply with these instructions will result in the application for relief not being considered unless the applicant demonstrates that such failure was the result of good cause. 8 C.F.R. § 1003.47(d).

In all cases in which the respondent is represented, the practitioner of record should ensure that the respondent understands the DHS biometrics instructions and the consequences of failing to timely comply with the instructions.

(2) **Detained cases** — If background and security investigations are required for detained respondents, DHS is responsible for timely fingerprinting the respondent and obtaining all necessary information. See 8 C.F.R. § 1003.47(d).

(l) Asylum Clock — The immigration court operates an asylum adjudications clock which measures the length of time an asylum application has been pending for each asylum applicant in removal proceedings. The asylum clock is an administrative function that tracks the number of days elapsed since the application was filed, not including any delays requested or caused by the applicant and ending with the final administrative adjudication of the application. This period also does not include administrative appeal or remand.

Certain asylum applicants are eligible to receive employment authorization from the Department of Homeland Security (DHS) 180 days after the application is filed, not including delays in the proceedings caused by the applicant. To facilitate DHS's adjudication of employment authorization applications, the Executive Office for Immigration Review (EOIR) provides DHS with access to its asylum adjudications clock for cases pending before EOIR. See INA §§ 208(d)(2), 208(d)(5)(A)(iii); 8 C.F.R. § 208.7.

(m) Waivers of Appearances — Respondents and practitioners of record must appear at all master calendar hearings unless the immigration judge has granted a waiver of appearance for that hearing. Waivers of appearances for master calendar hearings are described in subsections (1) and (2), below. Respondents and practitioners of record requesting waivers of appearances should note the limitations on waivers of appearances described in subsection (3), below.

Practitioners of record should note that a motion for a waiver of a practitioner's appearance is distinct from a practitioner's motion for a telephonic appearance. Motions for telephonic appearances are described in subsection (n), below.

(1) Waiver of practitioner of record's appearance — A practitioner of record's appearance at a master calendar hearing may be waived only by written motion filed in conjunction with written pleadings. See subsection (j), above. The written motion should be filed with a cover page labeled "MOTION TO WAIVE PRACTITIONER OF RECORD'S APPEARANCE" and comply with the deadlines and requirements for filing. See Chapter 3 (Filing with the Immigration Court), Appendix E (Cover Pages). The motion should state the date and time of the master calendar hearing and explain the reason(s) for requesting a waiver of the practitioner's appearance.

(2) Waiver of respondent's appearance — A respondent's appearance at a master calendar hearing may be waived by oral or written motion. See 8 C.F.R. § 1003.25(a). If in writing, the motion should be filed with a cover page labeled "MOTION TO WAIVE RESPONDENT'S APPEARANCE" and comply with the deadlines and requirements for filing. See Chapter 3 (Filing with the Immigration Court), Appendix E (Cover Pages). The motion should state the date and time of the master calendar hearing and explain the reason(s) for requesting a waiver of the respondent's appearance.

(3) Limitations on waivers of appearances

(A) Waivers granted separately — A waiver of a practitioner of record's appearance at a master calendar hearing does not constitute a waiver of the respondent's appearance. A waiver of a respondent's appearance at a master calendar hearing does not constitute a waiver of the practitioner of record's appearance.

(B) Pending motion — The mere filing of a motion to waive the appearance of a practitioner of record or respondent at a master calendar hearing does not excuse the appearance of the practitioner of record or respondent at that hearing. Therefore, the practitioner of record or respondent must appear in person unless the motion has been granted.

(C) Future hearings — A waiver of the appearance of a practitioner of record or respondent at a master calendar hearing does not constitute a waiver of the appearance of the practitioner of record or respondent at any future hearing.

(n) Telephonic Appearances — In certain instances, respondents and practitioners of record may appear by telephone at some master calendar hearings at the immigration judge's discretion. For more information, parties should contact the immigration court.

An appearance by telephone may be requested by written or oral motion. If in writing, the motion should be filed with a cover page labeled "MOTION TO PERMIT TELEPHONIC APPEARANCE" and comply with the deadlines and requirements for filing. See Chapter 3 (Filing with the Immigration Court), Appendix E (Cover Pages). The motion should state the date and time of the master calendar hearing and explain the reason(s) for requesting a telephonic appearance. In addition, the motion should state the telephone number of the practitioner of record or respondent.

Parties requesting an appearance by telephone should note the guidelines in subsections (1) through (5), below.

(1) Practitioner of record's telephonic appearance is not a waiver of respondent's appearance — Permission for a practitioner of record to appear by telephone at a master calendar hearing does not constitute a waiver of the respondent's appearance at that hearing. A request for a waiver of a respondent's appearance at a master calendar hearing must comply with the guidelines in subsection (m), above.

(2) Availability — A practitioner of record or respondent appearing by telephone must be available during the entire master calendar hearing.

(3) Cellular telephones — Unless expressly permitted by the immigration judge, cellular telephones should not be used for telephonic appearances.

(4) Pending motion — The mere filing of a motion to permit a practitioner of record or respondent to appear by telephone at a master calendar hearing does not excuse the appearance in person at that hearing by the practitioner of record or respondent. Therefore, the practitioner of record or respondent must appear in person unless the motion has been granted.

(5) Future hearings — Permission for a practitioner of record or respondent to appear by telephone at a master calendar hearing does not constitute permission for the practitioner of record or respondent to appear by telephone at any future hearing.

(o) Other Requests — In preparation for an upcoming individual calendar hearing, the following requests may be made at the master calendar hearing or afterwards, as described below.

(1) Interpreters — If a party anticipates that an interpreter will be needed at the individual calendar hearing, the party should request an interpreter, either by oral motion at a master calendar hearing, by written motion, or in a written pleading. Parties are strongly encouraged to submit requests for interpreters at the master calendar hearing rather than following the hearing. A written motion to request an interpreter should be filed with a cover page labeled "MOTION TO REQUEST AN INTERPRETER," and comply with the deadlines and requirements for filing. See Chapter 3 (Filing with the Immigration Court), Appendix E (Cover Pages).

A request for an interpreter, whether made by oral motion, by written motion, or in a written pleading, should contain the following information:

- the name of the language requested, including any variations in spelling

- the specific dialect of the language, if applicable

- the geographical locations where such dialect is spoken, if applicable

- the identification of any other languages in which the respondent or witness is fluent

- any other appropriate information necessary for the selection of an interpreter

(2) Video testimony — In certain instances, witnesses may testify by video at the individual calendar hearing, at the immigration judge's discretion. Video testimony may be requested only by written motion. For more information, parties should contact the immigration court.

A written motion to request video testimony should be filed with a cover page labeled "MOTION TO PRESENT VIDEO TESTIMONY," and comply with the deadlines and requirements for filing. See Chapter 3 (Filing with the Immigration Court), Appendix E (Cover Pages). A motion to present video testimony must include an explanation of why the witness cannot appear in person. In addition, parties wishing to present video testimony must comply with the requirements for witness lists. See Chapter 3.3(g) (Witness Lists).

If video testimony is permitted, the immigration judge specifies the time and manner under which the testimony is taken.

(3) Telephonic testimony — In certain instances, witnesses may testify by telephone, at the immigration judge's discretion. If a party wishes to have witnesses testify by telephone at the individual calendar hearing, this may be requested by oral motion at the master calendar hearing or by written motion. If telephonic testimony is permitted, the court specifies the time and manner under which the testimony is taken. For more information, parties should contact the immigration court.

A written motion to request telephonic testimony should be filed with a cover page labeled "MOTION TO PRESENT TELEPHONIC TESTIMONY," and comply with the deadlines and requirements for filing. See Chapter 3 (Filing with the Immigration Court), Appendix E (Cover Pages). In addition, parties wishing to present telephonic testimony must comply with the requirements for witness lists. See Chapter 3.3(g) (Witness Lists).

(A) Contents — An oral or written motion to permit telephonic testimony must include:

- an explanation of why the witness cannot appear in person

- the witness's telephone number and the location from which the witness will testify

(B) Availability — A witness appearing by telephone must be available to testify at any time during the course of the individual calendar hearing.

(C) Cellular telephones — Unless permitted by the immigration judge, cellular telephones should not be used by witnesses testifying telephonically.

(D) International calls — If international telephonic testimony is permitted, the requesting party should bring a pre-paid telephone card to the immigration court to pay for the call.

(p) Adjournment — The immigration judge may adjourn a hearing as necessary. See Appendix O (Adjournment Codes) providing adjournment, call-up, and case identification codes used to track case information in EOIR's case management system.

4.16   Individual Calendar Hearing

(a) Generally — Evidentiary hearings on contested matters are referred to as individual calendar hearings or merits hearings. Contested matters include challenges to removability and applications for relief.

(b) Filings — The following documents should be filed in preparation for the individual calendar hearing, as necessary. Parties should note that, since Records of Proceedings in removal proceedings are kept separate from Records of Proceedings in bond redetermination proceedings, documents already filed in bond redetermination proceedings must be re-filed for removal proceedings. See Chapter 9.3 (Bond Proceedings).

(1) Applications, exhibits, motions — Parties should file all applications for relief, proposed exhibits, and motions, as appropriate. All submissions must comply with the deadlines and requirements for filing. See Chapter 3 (Filing with the Immigration Court).

(2) Witness list — If presenting witnesses other than the respondent, parties must file a witness list that complies with the requirements of Chapter 3.3(g) (Witness Lists). In addition, the witness list must comply with the deadlines and requirements for filing. See Chapter 3 (Filing with the Immigration Court).

(3) Criminal history chart — When submitting documents relating to a respondent's criminal arrests, prosecutions, or convictions, parties are encouraged to use a criminal history chart and attach all pertinent documentation, such as arrest and conviction records. For guidance on submitting a criminal history chart, see Chapter 3.3(f) (Criminal Conviction Documents). For a sample, see Appendix M (Sample Criminal History Chart). Parties submitting a criminal history chart should comply with the deadlines and requirements for filing. See Chapter 3 (Filing with the Immigration Court).

(c) Opening the Individual Calendar Hearing — The immigration judge turns on the recording equipment at the beginning of the individual calendar hearing. The hearing is recorded, except for off-the-record discussions. See Chapter 4.10 (Record).

On the record, the immigration judge identifies the type of proceeding being conducted (e.g., a removal proceeding); the respondent's name and A-number; the date, time, and place of the proceeding; and the presence of the parties. The immigration judge also verifies the respondent's name, address, and telephone number. If the respondent's address or telephone number have changed, the respondent must submit a change of address form (Form EOIR-33 Change of Address/Contact Information Form).

If the respondent is requesting relief that requires background investigations and security checks, the immigration judge inquires, on the record, whether DHS completed them. If they are completed, the immigration judge must ensure to note the name of the DHS counsel who reported the completeness and the date on the Immigration Judge Worksheet. If the background investigations and security checks are incomplete due to the respondent's lack of compliance without good cause, the immigration judge may deem the application for the covered form of relief abandoned and enter an order dismissing the application. 8 C.F.R. § 1003.47(c).

If the background investigations and security checks were not completed due to DHS, DHS may seek a continuance. Additionally, the immigration judge may proceed with the merits hearing; while they can deny relief, they cannot render a decision granting any covered form of relief until the background investigations and security checks are complete. 8 C.F.R. §§ 1003.47(f), 1003.47(g). If, after hearing the merits of the case, the immigration judge would grant covered relief, they must reschedule the matter for a date when DHS believes the background investigations and security checks will be complete. If, in the meantime, they decide to write a draft opinion, they must not discuss its existence or content with either party.

If relief is granted that entitles the respondent to a document from DHS, the immigration judge's decision must include an advisal to the respondent that they will need to contact an appropriate office of DHS to obtain a new document. 8 C.F.R. § 1003.47(i).

(d) Conduct of Hearing — While the immigration judge decides how each hearing is conducted, parties should be prepared to:

- make an opening statement

- raise any objections to the other party's evidence

- present witnesses and evidence on all issues

- cross-examine opposing witnesses and object to testimony

- make a closing statement

(e) Witnesses — All witnesses, including the respondent if they testify, are placed under oath by the immigration judge before testifying. If necessary, an interpreter is provided. See Chapters 4.11 (Interpreters), 4.15(o) (Other Requests). The immigration judge may ask questions of the respondent and all witnesses at any time during the hearing. See INA § 240(b)(1).

(f) Pro Se Respondents — Unrepresented ("pro se") respondents have the same hearing rights and obligations as represented respondents. For example, pro se respondents may testify, present witnesses, cross-examine any witnesses presented by the Department of Homeland Security (DHS), and object to evidence presented by DHS. When a respondent appears pro se, the immigration judge generally participates in questioning the respondent and the respondent's witnesses. As in all removal proceedings, DHS may object to evidence presented by a pro se respondent and may cross-examine the respondent and the respondent's witnesses.

(g) Decision — After the parties have presented their cases, the immigration judge renders a decision. The immigration judge may render an oral decision at the hearing's conclusion, or they may render an oral or written decision on a later date. See Chapter 1.4(c) (Immigration Judge Decisions). If the decision is rendered orally, the parties are given a signed summary order from the court.

(h) Appeal — The respondent and the Department of Homeland Security have the right to appeal the immigration judge's decision to the Board of Immigration Appeals. See Chapter 6 (Appeals of Immigration Judge Decisions). A party may waive the right to appeal. At the conclusion of immigration court proceedings, the immigration judge informs the parties of the deadline for filing an appeal with the Board, unless the right to appeal is waived. See Chapter 6.4 (Waiver of Appeal).

Parties should note that the immigration judge may ask the Board to review the immigration judge's decision. This is known as "certifying" a case to the Board. The certification of a case is separate from any appeal in the case. Therefore, a party wishing to appeal must file an appeal *even if* the immigration judge has certified the case to the Board. See Chapter 6.5 (Certification).

If an appeal is not filed, the immigration judge's decision becomes the final administrative decision in the matter, unless the case has been certified to the Board.

(i) Relief Granted — If a respondent's application for relief from removal is granted, the respondent is provided the Department of Homeland Security (DHS) post-order instructions. These instructions describe the steps the respondent should follow to obtain documentation of their immigration status from U.S. Citizenship and Immigration Services, a component of DHS.

More information about these post-order instructions can be found by searching for "post-order instructions" on the U.S. Citizenship and Immigration Services website.

For respondents who are granted asylum, information on asylees' benefits and responsibilities is available at the immigration court.

(j) Adjournment — The immigration judge may adjourn a hearing as necessary. See Appendix O (Adjournment Codes) providing adjournment, call-up, and case identification codes used to track case information in EOIR's case management system.

4.17 In Absentia Hearing

(a) In General — Any delay in the respondent's appearance at a master calendar or individual calendar hearing may result in the respondent being ordered removed "in absentia" (in the respondent's absence). See 8 C.F.R. § 1003.26(c). See also Chapter 4.8 (Attendance). There is no appeal from a removal order issued in absentia. However, parties may file a motion to reopen to rescind an in absentia removal order. See Chapter 5.9 (Motions to Reopen In Absentia Orders).

(b) Deportation and Exclusion Proceedings — Parties should note that in absentia orders in deportation and exclusion proceedings are governed by different standards than in absentia orders in removal proceedings. For the provisions governing in absentia orders in deportation and exclusion proceedings, see 8 C.F.R. § 1003.26. See also Chapter 7 (Other Proceedings before Immigration Judges).

4.18   Pre-Hearing Conferences and Statements

(a) Pre-hearing Conferences — Pre-hearing conferences are held between the parties and the immigration judge to narrow issues, obtain stipulations between the parties, exchange information voluntarily, and otherwise simplify and organize the proceeding. See 8 C.F.R. § 1003.21(a).

Pre-hearing conferences may be requested by a party or initiated by the immigration judge. A party's request for a pre-hearing conference may be made orally or by written motion. If in writing, the motion should be filed with a cover page labeled "MOTION FOR A PRE-HEARING CONFERENCE," and comply with the deadlines and requirements for filing. See Chapter 3 (Filing with the Immigration Court), Appendix E (Cover Pages).

Even if a pre-hearing conference is not held, the parties are strongly encouraged to confer prior to a hearing in order to narrow issues for litigation. Parties are further encouraged to file pre-hearing statements following such discussions. See subsection (b), below.

(b) Pre-hearing Statements — An immigration judge may order the parties to file a pre-hearing statement. See 8 C.F.R. § 1003.21(b). Parties are encouraged to file a pre-hearing statement even if not ordered to do so by the immigration judge. Parties also are encouraged to file pre-hearing briefs addressing questions of law. See Chapter 4.19 (Pre-Hearing Briefs).

> **(1) Filing** — A pre-hearing statement should be filed with a cover page with an appropriate label (e.g., "PARTIES' PRE-HEARING STATEMENT"), and comply with the deadlines and requirements for filing. See Chapter 3 (Filing with the Immigration Court), Appendix E (Cover Pages).

> **(2) Contents of a pre-hearing statement** — In general, the purpose of a pre-hearing statement is to narrow and reduce the factual and legal issues in advance of an individual calendar hearing. For example, a pre-hearing statement may include the following items:

> - a statement of facts to which both parties have stipulated, together with a statement that the parties have communicated in good faith to stipulate to the fullest extent possible

> - a list of proposed witnesses and what they will establish

- a list of exhibits, copies of exhibits to be introduced, and a statement of the reason for their introduction

- the estimated time required to present the case

- a statement of unresolved issues in the proceeding

See 8 C.F.R. § 1003.21(b).

4.19 Pre-Hearing Briefs

(a) Generally — An immigration judge may order the parties to file pre-hearing briefs. Parties are encouraged to file pre-hearing briefs even if not ordered to do so by the immigration judge. Parties are also encouraged to file pre-hearing statements to narrow and reduce the legal and factual issues in dispute. See Chapter 4.18(b) (Pre-Hearing Statements).

(b) Guidelines — Pre-hearing briefs advise the immigration judge of a party's positions and arguments on questions of law. A well-written pre-hearing brief is in the party's best interest and is of great importance to the immigration judge. Pre-hearing briefs should be clear, concise, and well-organized. They should cite the record, as appropriate. Pre-hearing briefs should cite legal authorities fully, fairly, and accurately.

Pre-hearing briefs should always recite those facts that are appropriate and germane to the adjudication of the issue(s) at the individual calendar hearing. They should cite proper legal authority, where such authority is available. See subsection (f), below. Pre-hearing briefs should not belabor facts or law that are not in dispute. Parties are encouraged to expressly identify in their pre-hearing briefs those facts or law that are not in dispute.

Briefs and other submissions should always be paginated. Parties must limit the body of their briefs to 25 pages. If a party believes it cannot adequately address the issues in the case within the page limit, the party may make a motion to increase the page limit. Pre-hearing briefs should always be paginated.

(c) Format

(1) Filing — Pre-hearing briefs should be filed with a cover page with an appropriate label (e.g., "RESPONDENT'S PRE-HEARING BRIEF"), and comply with the deadlines and requirements for filing. See Chapter 3 (Filing with the Immigration Court), Appendix E (Cover Pages). Pre-hearing briefs must be signed by a pro se respondent, a respondent's practitioner of record, or a representative of the Department of Homeland Security. See Chapter 3.3(b) (Signatures). See also Chapter 2 (Appearances before the Immigration Court).

(2) Contents — Unless otherwise directed by the immigration judge, the following items should be included in a pre-hearing brief:

- a concise statement of facts

- a statement of issues

- a statement of the burden of proof

- a summary of the argument

- the argument

- a short conclusion stating the precise relief or remedy sought

(3) Statement of facts — Statements of facts in pre-hearing briefs should be concise. Facts should be set out clearly. Points of contention and points of agreement should be expressly identified.

Facts, like case law, require citation. Parties should support factual assertions by citing to any supporting documentation or exhibits, whether in the record or accompanying the brief. See subsection (f), below.

Do not misstate or misrepresent the facts or omit unfavorable facts that are relevant to the legal issue. A brief's accuracy and integrity are paramount to the persuasiveness of the argument and the decision regarding the legal issue(s) addressed in the brief.

(4) Footnotes — Substantive arguments should be restricted to the text of pre-hearing briefs. The excessive use of footnotes is discouraged.

(5) Headings and other markers — Pre-hearing briefs should employ headings, sub-headings, and spacing to make the brief more readable. Short paragraphs with topic sentences and proper headings facilitate the coherence and cohesiveness of arguments.

(6) Chronologies — Pre-hearing briefs should contain a chronology of the facts, especially where the facts are complicated or involve several events. Charts or similar graphic representations that chronicle events are welcome. See Appendix M (Sample Criminal History Chart).

(d) Consolidated Pre-Hearing Briefs — Where cases have been consolidated, one pre-hearing brief may be submitted on behalf of all respondents in the consolidated proceeding, provided that each respondent's full name and A-number appear on the consolidated pre-hearing brief. See Chapter 4.21 (Combining and Separating Cases).

(e) Responses to Pre-Hearing Briefs — When a party files a pre-hearing brief, the other party may file a response brief. A response brief should be filed with a cover page with an appropriate label (e.g., "DHS RESPONSE TO PRE-HEARING BRIEF"), and comply with the deadlines and requirements for filing. See Chapter 3 (Filing with the Immigration Court), Appendix E (Cover Pages). Response briefs should comply with the guidelines for pre-hearing briefs set forth above.

(f) Citation — Parties are expected to provide complete and clear citations to all factual and legal authorities. Parties should comply with the citation guidelines in Appendix I (Citations).

4.20   Subpoenas

(a) **Applying for a Subpoena** — A party may request that a subpoena be issued requiring that witnesses attend a hearing or that documents be produced. See 8 C.F.R. §§ 1003.35, 1287.4(a)(2)(ii). A request for a subpoena may be made by written motion or by oral motion. If made in writing, the request should be filed with a cover page labeled "MOTION FOR SUBPOENA," and comply with the deadlines and requirements for filing. See Chapter 3 (Filing with the Immigration Court), Appendix E (Cover Pages). Whether made orally or in writing, a motion for a subpoena must:

- provide the court with a proposed subpoena

- state what the party expects to prove by such witnesses or documentary evidence

- show affirmatively that the party has made diligent effort, without success, to produce the witnesses or documentary evidence

If requesting a subpoena for telephonic testimony, the party should also comply with Chapter 4.15(o)(3) (Telephonic Testimony).

(b) **Contents** — A proposed subpoena should contain:

- the respondent's name and A-number

- the type of proceeding

- the name and address of the person to whom the subpoena is directed

- a command that the recipient of the subpoena:

    o   testify in court at a specified time,

    o   testify by telephone at a specified time, or

    o   produce specified books, papers, or other items

- a return on service of subpoena

See 8 C.F.R. § 1003.35(b)(3).

(c) **Appearance of Witness** — If the witness whose testimony is required is more than 100 miles from the immigration court where the hearing is being conducted, the subpoena must provide for the witness's appearance at the immigration court nearest to the witness to respond to oral or written interrogatories, unless the party calling the witness has no objection to bringing the witness to the hearing. See 8 C.F.R. § 1003.35(b)(4).

(d) **Service** — A subpoena issued under the above provisions may be served by any person over 18 years of age not a party to the case. See 8 C.F.R. § 1003.35(b)(5).

4.21   Combining and Separating Cases

(a) **Consolidated Cases** — Consolidation of cases is the administrative joining of separate cases into a single adjudication for all of the parties involved. Consolidation is generally limited to cases involving immediate family members. The immigration court may consolidate cases at its discretion or upon motion of one or both of the parties, where appropriate. For example, the immigration court may grant consolidation when spouses or siblings have separate but overlapping circumstances or claims for relief. Consolidation must be sought through the filing of a written motion that states the reasons for requesting consolidation. Such motion should include a cover page labeled "MOTION FOR CONSOLIDATION" and comply with the deadlines and requirements for filing. See Chapter 3 (Filing with the Immigration Court), Appendix E (Cover Pages). A copy of the motion should be filed for each case included in the request for consolidation. The motion should be filed as far in advance of any filing deadline as possible. See Chapter 3.1(b) (Timing of Submissions).

    (b) Severance of Cases — Severance of cases is the division of a consolidated case into separate cases, relative to each individual. The immigration court may sever cases in its discretion or upon request of one or both of the parties. Severance must be sought through the filing of a written motion that states the reasons for requesting severance. Such motion should include a cover page labeled "MOTION FOR SEVERANCE" and comply with the deadlines and requirements for filing. See Chapter 3 (Filing with the Immigration Court), Appendix E (Cover Pages). A copy of the motion should be filed for each case included in the request for severance. Parties are advised, however, that such motion should be filed as far in advance of any filing deadline as possible. See Chapter 3.1(b) (Timing of Submissions).

4.22   Juveniles

    (a) Scheduling — Immigration courts do their best to schedule cases involving unaccompanied juveniles on a separate docket or at a fixed time in the week or month, separate and apart from adult cases.

    (b) Representation — An immigration judge cannot appoint a practitioner or guardian ad litem for unaccompanied juveniles. However, the Executive Office for Immigration Review encourages the use of pro bono legal resources for unaccompanied juveniles. For further information, see Chapter 2.2(b) (List of Pro Bono Legal Service Providers).

    (c) Courtroom Orientation — Juveniles are encouraged, under the supervision of court personnel, to explore an empty courtroom, sit in all locations, and practice answering simple questions before the hearing. The Department of Health and Human Services, Office of Refugee Resettlement, provides orientation for most juveniles in their native languages, explaining immigration court proceedings.

    (d) Courtroom Modifications — Immigration judges make reasonable modifications for juveniles. These may include allowing juveniles to bring pillows, or toys, permitting juveniles to sit with an adult companion, and permitting juveniles to testify outside the witness stand next to a trusted adult or friend.

    (e) Detained Juveniles — For additional provisions regarding detained juveniles, see Chapter 9.2 (Detained Juveniles).

This page intentionally left blank.

Chapter 5 Motions before the Immigration Court

5.1   Who May File

(a) **Parties** — Only a respondent who is in proceedings before the immigration court (or the respondent's practitioner of record), or the Department of Homeland Security may file a motion. A motion must identify all parties covered by the motion and state clearly their full names and A-numbers, including all family members in proceedings. See Chapter 5.2(b) (Form), Appendix E (Cover Pages). The immigration judge will *not* assume that the motion includes all family members (or group members in consolidated proceedings). See Chapter 4.21 (Combining and Separating Cases).

(b) **Practitioners of Record** — Whenever a party is represented, the party should submit all motions to the Court through the practitioner of record. See 8 C.F.R. §§ 1003.17(a)(2), 1292.5(a), Chapter 2.1(b)(7) (Filing After Entry of Appearance as Practitioner of Record).

(1) **Pre-decision motions** — If a practitioner of record has already filed a Notice of Entry of Appearance as Attorney or Representative Before the Immigration Court (Form EOIR-28), and the immigration judge has not rendered a final order in the case, a motion need not be accompanied by a Form EOIR-28. However, if a practitioner of record is appearing for the first time, the practitioner must file a Form EOIR-28 along with the motion. See Chapter 2 (Appearances before the Immigration Court).

(2) **Post-decision motions** — All motions to reopen, motions to reconsider, and motions to reopen to rescind an in absentia order drafted or prepared by a practitioner must be accompanied by a Form EOIR-28 or Form EOIR-61. If accompanied by a Form EOIR-28, the practitioner will be the practitioner of record on the motion and proceedings subsequent to the motion, if any. See Chapter 2 (Appearances before the Immigration Court).

(c) **Persons not Party to the Proceedings** — Only a party to a proceeding, a practitioner of record, or a practitioner who drafted, completed, or prepared the document(s) pursuant to a limited appearance for document assistance may file a motion pertaining to that proceeding. Family members, employers, and other third parties may not file a motion. If a third party seeks immigration court action in a particular case, the request should be made through a party to the proceeding.

5.2   Filing a Motion

(a) **Where to File** — The immigration court may entertain motions only in those cases in which it has jurisdiction. See subsections (1), (2), (3), below, Appendix J (Filing Motions). If the immigration court has jurisdiction, motions are filed with the immigration court having administrative control over the Record of Proceedings. See Chapter 3.1(a) (Filing).

(1) **Cases not yet filed with the immigration court** — Except for requests for bond redetermination proceedings, the immigration court cannot entertain motions if a charging document (i.e., a Notice to Appear) has not been

filed with the Court. See Chapters 4.2 (Commencement of Removal Proceedings), 9.3(b) (Jurisdiction).

(2) Cases pending before the immigration court — If a charging document has been filed with the immigration court but the case has not yet been decided by the immigration judge, all motions must be filed with the Court.

(3) Cases already decided by the immigration court —

(A) No appeal filed — Where a case has been decided by the immigration judge, and no appeal has been filed with the Board of Immigration Appeals, motions to reopen and motions to reconsider are filed with the immigration court. Parties should be mindful of the strict time and number limits on motions to reopen and motions to reconsider. See Chapters 5.7 (Motions to Reopen), 5.8 (Motions to Reconsider), 5.9 (Motions to Reopen In Absentia Orders).

(B) Appeal filed — Where a case has been decided by the immigration judge, and an appeal has been filed with the Board of Immigration Appeals, the parties should consult the Board of Immigration Appeals Practice Manual. See also Appendix J (Filing Motions).

(b) Form — There is no official form for filing a motion before the immigration court. Motions must be filed with a cover page and comply with the requirements for filing. See Chapter 3 (Filing with the Immigration Court), Appendix E (Cover Pages). In addition, all motions not filed through ECAS must be accompanied by the appropriate proposed order for the immigration judge's signature. Motions and supporting documents should be assembled in the order described in Chapter 3.3(c)(1) (Order of documents).

A motion's cover page must accurately describe the motion. See Chapter 3.3(c)(6) (Cover page and caption). Parties should note that the immigration court construes motions according to content rather than title. Therefore, the court applies time and number limits according to the nature of the motion rather than the motion's title. See Chapter 5.3 (Motion Limits).

Motions must state with particularity the grounds on which the motion is based. In addition, motions must identify the relief or remedy sought by the filing party.

(c) When to File — Pre-decision motions must comply with the deadlines for filing discussed in Chapter 3.1(b) (Timing of Submissions). Deadlines for filing motions to reopen, motions to reconsider, and motions to reopen in absentia orders are governed by statute or regulation. See Chapters 5.7 (Motions to Reopen), 5.8 (Motions to Reconsider), 5.9 (Motions to Reopen In Absentia Orders).

(d) Copy of Underlying Order — Motions to reopen and motions to reconsider should be accompanied by a copy of the immigration judge's decision, where available.

(e) Evidence — Statements made in a motion are *not* evidence. If a motion is based upon evidence that was not made part of the record by the immigration judge, that evidence should be submitted with the motion. Such evidence may include sworn affidavits, declarations under the penalties of perjury, and documentary evidence. The immigration court will not suspend or delay adjudication of a motion pending the receipt of supplemental evidence.

All evidence submitted with a motion must comply with the requirements of Chapter 3.3 (Documents).

(f) Filing Fee — Where the motion requires a filing fee, the motion must be accompanied by a fee receipt from the Department of Homeland Security (DHS) or a request that the immigration judge waive the fee. Filing fees are paid to DHS. See Chapter 3.4 (Filing Fees).

(g) Application for Relief — A motion based upon eligibility for relief must be accompanied by a copy of the application for that relief and all supporting documents if an application is normally required. See 8 C.F.R. § 1003.23(b)(3). A grant of a motion based on eligibility for relief does not constitute a grant of the underlying application for relief.

The application for relief must be duly completed and executed, in accordance with the requirements for such relief. The original application for relief should be held by the filing party for submission to the immigration court, if appropriate, after the ruling on the motion. See Chapter 11.3 (Submitting Completed Forms). The copy that is submitted to the immigration court should be accompanied by a copy of the appropriate supporting documents.

If a certain form of relief requires an application, *prima facie eligibility for that relief cannot be shown without it.* For example, if a motion to reopen is based on adjustment of status, a copy of the completed Application to Adjust Status (Form I-485) should be filed *with* the motion, along with the necessary documents.

Application fees are *not* paid to the immigration court and should not accompany the motion. Fees for applications should be paid if and when the motion is granted in accordance with the filing procedures for that application. See Chapter 3.4(c) (Application Fees).

(h) Visa Petitions — If a motion is based on an application for adjustment of status and there is an underlying visa petition that has been approved, a copy of the visa petition and the approval notice should accompany the motion. When a petition is subject to visa availability, evidence that a visa is immediately available should also accompany the motion (e.g., a copy of the State Department's Visa Bulletin reflecting that the priority date is "current").

If a motion is based on adjustment of status and the underlying visa petition has not yet been adjudicated, a copy of that visa petition, all supporting documents, and the filing receipt (Form I-797) should accompany the motion.

Parties should note that, in certain instances, an approved visa petition is required for motions based on adjustment of status. See, e.g., *Matter of H-A-*, 22 I&N Dec. 728 (BIA 1999), modified by *Matter of Velarde*, 23 I&N Dec. 253 (BIA 2002).

Filing fees for visa petitions are not paid to the immigration court and should not accompany the motion. The filing fee for a visa petition is submitted to DHS when the petition is filed with DHS.

(i) Opposing Party's Position — The party filing a motion should make a good faith effort to ascertain the opposing party's position on the motion. The opposing party's position should be stated in the motion. If the filing party was unable to ascertain the opposing party's position, a description of the efforts made to contact the opposing party should be included.

(j) Oral Argument — The immigration court generally does not grant requests for oral argument on a motion. If the immigration judge determines that oral argument is necessary, the parties are notified of the hearing date.

5.3   Motion Limits

Certain motions are limited in time (when the motions must be filed) and number (how many motions may be filed). Pre-decision motions are limited in time. See Chapter 3.1(b) (Timing of Submissions). Motions to reopen and motions to reconsider are limited in both time and number. See Chapters 5.7 (Motions to Reopen), 5.8 (Motions to Reconsider), 5.9 (Motions to Reopen In Absentia Orders). Time and number limits are strictly enforced.

5.4   Multiple Motions

When multiple motions are filed, the motions should be accompanied by a cover letter listing the separate motions. In addition, each motion must include a cover page and comply with the deadlines and requirements for filing. See Chapter 5.2(b) (Form), Appendix E (Cover Pages).

Parties are strongly discouraged from filing compound motions, which are motions that combine two separate requests. Parties should note that time and number limits apply to motions even when submitted as part of a compound motion. For example, if a motion seeks both reopening and reconsideration, and is filed more than 30 days after the immigration judge's decision (the deadline for reconsideration) but within 90 days of that decision (the deadline for reopening), the portion that seeks reconsideration is considered untimely.

5.5   Motion Briefs

A brief is not required in support of a motion. However, if a brief is filed, it should accompany the motion. See 8 C.F.R. § 1003.23(b)(1)(ii). In general, motion briefs should comply with the requirements of Chapters 3.3 (Documents) and 4.19 (Pre-Hearing Briefs).

A brief filed in opposition to a motion must comply with the filing deadlines for responses. See Chapter 3.1(b) (Timing of Submissions).

5.6   Transcript Requests

The immigration court does not prepare a transcript of proceedings.
See Chapter 4.10 (Record) Parties are reminded that recordings of proceedings are

generally available for review by prior arrangement with the immigration court. See Chapter 1.5(c) (Records).

5.7   Motions to Reopen

(a) Purpose — A motion to reopen asks the immigration court to reopen proceedings after the immigration judge has rendered a decision, so that the immigration judge can consider new facts or evidence in the case.

(b) Requirements —

(1) Filing — The motion should be filed with a cover page labeled "MOTION TO REOPEN" and comply with the deadlines and requirements for filing. See subsection (c), below, Chapter 5.2 (Filing a Motion), Appendix E (Cover Pages). If the respondent is represented by a practitioner of record or has received document assistance from a practitioner, the motion must be accompanied by a Form EOIR-28 or Form EOIR-61. See Chapter 2.1. (Representation and Appearances Generally). To ensure that the immigration court has the respondent's current address, a change of address form (EOIR-33/IC) should be filed with the motion. Depending on the nature of the motion, a filing fee or fee waiver request may be required. See Chapter 3.4 (Filing Fees). If the motion is based on eligibility for relief, the motion must be accompanied by a copy of the application for that relief and all supporting documents, if an application is normally required. See Chapter 5.2(g) (Application for Relief).

(2) Content — A motion to reopen must state the new facts that will be proven at a reopened hearing if the motion is granted, and the motion must be supported by affidavits or other evidentiary material. 8 C.F.R. § 1003.23(b)(3).

A motion to reopen is not granted unless it appears to the immigration judge that the evidence offered is material and was not available and could not have been discovered or presented at an earlier stage in the proceedings. See 8 C.F.R. § 1003.23(b)(3).

A motion to reopen based on an application for relief will not be granted if it appears the respondent's right to apply for that relief was fully explained and the respondent had an opportunity to apply for that relief at an earlier stage in the proceedings (unless the relief is sought on the basis of circumstances that have arisen subsequent to that stage of the proceedings). 8 C.F.R. § 1003.23(b)(3).

(c) Time Limits — As a general rule, a motion to reopen must be filed within 90 days of an immigration judge's final order. 8 C.F.R. § 1003.23(b)(1). (For cases decided by the immigration judge before July 1, 1996, the motion to reopen was due on or before September 30, 1996. 8 C.F.R. § 1003.23(b)(1). There are few exceptions. See subsection (e), below.

Responses to motions to reopen are due within ten (10) days after the motion was received by the immigration court, unless otherwise specified by the immigration judge.

(d) Number Limits — A party is permitted only one motion to reopen. 8 C.F.R. § 1003.23(b)(1). There are few exceptions. See subsection (e), below.

(e) Exceptions to the Limits on Motions to Reopen — A motion to reopen may be filed outside the time and number limits only in specific circumstances. See 8 C.F.R. § 1003.23(b)(4).

(1) Changed circumstances — The time and numerical limitations do not apply to a motion to reopen based on a request for asylum, withholding of removal ("restriction on removal"), or protection under the Convention Against Torture, that is premised on changed country conditions arising in the country of nationality or the country to which removal has been ordered, if such evidence is material and was not available and could not have been discovered or presented at the previous proceeding. See 8 C.F.R. § 1003.23(b)(4)(i). Motions based on changed circumstances must also be accompanied by evidence of the changed circumstances alleged. See 8 C.F.R. § 1003.23(b)(3).

(2) In absentia proceedings — There are special rules pertaining to motions to reopen following a respondent's failure to appear for a hearing. See Chapter 5.9 (Motions to Reopen In Absentia Orders).

(3) Joint motions — Motions to reopen that are agreed upon by all parties and are jointly filed are not limited in time or number. See 8 C.F.R. § 1003.23(b)(4)(iv).

(4) DHS motions — For cases in removal proceedings, the Department of Homeland Security (DHS) is not subject to time and number limits on motions to reopen. See 8 C.F.R. § 1003.23(b)(1). For cases brought in deportation or exclusion proceedings, DHS is subject to the time and number limits on motions to reopen, unless the basis of the motion is fraud in the original proceeding or a crime that would support termination of asylum. See 8 C.F.R. § 1003.23(b)(1).

(5) Pre-9/30/96 motions — Motions filed before September 30, 1996, do not count toward the one-motion limit.

(6) Battered spouses, children, and parents — There are special rules for certain motions to reopen by battered spouses, children, and parents. INA § 240(c)(7)(C)(iv).

(7) Other — In addition to the regulatory exceptions for motions to reopen, exceptions may be created in accordance with special statutes, case law, directives, or other special legal circumstances. The immigration judge may also reopen proceedings at any time on their own motion. See 8 C.F.R. § 1003.23(b)(1).

(f) Evidence — A motion to reopen must be supported by evidence. See Chapter 5.2(e) (Evidence).

(g) Motions Filed Prior to Deadline for Appeal — A motion to reopen filed prior to the deadline for filing an appeal does not stay or extend the deadline for filing the appeal.

(h) Motions Filed While an Appeal is Pending — Once an appeal is filed with the Board of Immigration Appeals, the immigration judge no longer has jurisdiction over the case. See Chapter 5.2(a) (Where to File). Thus, motions to reopen should not be filed with the immigration court after an appeal is taken to the Board.

(i) Administratively Closed Cases — When proceedings have been administratively closed, the proper motion is a motion to recalendar, *not* a motion to reopen. See Chapter 5.10(u) (Motion to Recalendar).

(j) Automatic Stays — A motion to reopen that is filed with the immigration court does not automatically stay an order of removal or deportation. 8 C.F.R. § 1003.23(b)(1)(v); see also Chapter 8 (Stays). For automatic stay provisions for motions to reopen to rescind in absentia orders, see Chapter 5.9(d)(4) (Automatic stay).

(k) Criminal Convictions — A motion claiming that a criminal conviction has been overturned, vacated, modified, or disturbed in some way must be accompanied by clear evidence that the conviction has actually been disturbed. Thus, neither an intention to seek post-conviction relief nor the mere eligibility for post-conviction relief, by itself, is sufficient to reopen proceedings.

5.8   Motions to Reconsider

(a) Purpose — A motion to reconsider either identifies an error in law or fact in the immigration judge's prior decision or identifies a change in law that affects an immigration judge's prior decision and asks the immigration judge to reexamine their ruling. A motion to reconsider is based on the existing record and does not seek to introduce new facts or evidence.

(b) Requirements — The motion should be filed with a cover page labeled "MOTION TO RECONSIDER" and comply with the deadlines and requirements for filing. See subsection (c), below, Chapter 5.2 (Filing a Motion), Appendix E (Cover Pages). If the respondent is represented by a practitioner of record or has received document assistance from a practitioner, the motion must be accompanied by a Form EOIR-28 or Form EOIR-61. See Chapter 2.1 (Representation and Appearances Generally). To ensure that the immigration court has the respondent's current address, a change of address form (EOIR-33/IC) should be filed with the motion. A filing fee or a fee waiver request may be required. See Chapter 3.4 (Filing Fees).

(c) Time Limits — A motion to reconsider must be filed within 30 days of the immigration judge's final administrative order. 8 C.F.R. § 1003.23(b)(1). (For cases decided by the immigration court before July 1, 1996, the motion to reconsider was due on or before July 31, 1996. 8 C.F.R. § 1003.23(b)(1).

Responses to motions to reconsider are due within ten (10) days after the motion was received by the immigration court, unless otherwise specified by the immigration judge.

(d) Number Limits — As a general rule, a party may file only one motion to reconsider. See 8 C.F.R. § 1003.23(b)(1). Motions filed prior to July 31, 1996, do not count toward the one-motion limit. Although a party may file a motion to reconsider the denial of a motion to reopen, a party may not file a motion to reconsider the denial of a motion to reconsider. 8 C.F.R. § 1003.23(b)(1).

(e) Exceptions to the Limits on Motions to Reconsider —

(1) Respondent motions — There are no exceptions to the time and number limitations on motions to reconsider when filed by a respondent.

(2) DHS motions — For cases in removal proceedings, the Department of Homeland Security (DHS) is not subject to time and number limits on motions to reconsider. See 8 C.F.R. § 1003.23(b)(1). For cases brought in deportation or exclusion proceedings, DHS is subject to the time and number limits on motions to reconsider, unless the basis of the motion is fraud in the original proceeding or a crime that would support termination of asylum. See 8 C.F.R. § 1003.23(b)(1).

(3) Other — In addition to the regulatory exceptions for motions to reconsider, exceptions may be created in accordance with special statutes, case law, directives, or other special legal circumstances. The immigration judge may also reconsider proceedings at any time on its own motion. 8 C.F.R. § 1003.23(b)(1).

(f) Identification of Error — A motion to reconsider must state with particularity the errors of fact or law in the immigration judge's prior decision, with appropriate citation to authority and the record. If a motion to reconsider is premised upon changes in the law, the motion should identify the changes and, where appropriate, provide copies of that law. For citation guidelines, see Chapter 4.19(f) (Citation), Appendix I (Citations).

(g) Motions Filed Prior to Deadline for Appeal — A motion to reconsider filed prior to the deadline for filing an appeal does not stay or extend the deadline for filing the appeal.

(h) Motions Filed while an Appeal is Pending — Once an appeal is filed with the Board of Immigration Appeals, the immigration judge no longer has jurisdiction over the case. See Chapter 5.2(a) (Where to File). Thus, motions to reconsider should not be filed with an immigration judge after an appeal is taken to the Board.

(i) Automatic Stays — A motion to reconsider does not automatically stay an order of removal or deportation. See Chapter 8 (Stays).

(j) Criminal Convictions — When a criminal conviction has been overturned, vacated, modified, or disturbed in some way, the proper motion is a motion to reopen, not a motion to reconsider. See Chapter 5.7(k) (Criminal Convictions).

5.9   Motions to Reopen In Absentia Orders

(a) In General — A motion to reopen requesting that an in absentia order be rescinded asks the immigration judge to consider the reasons why the respondent did not appear at the respondent's scheduled hearing. See Chapter 4.17 (In Absentia Hearing).

(b) Filing — The motion should be filed with a cover page labeled "MOTION TO REOPEN AN IN ABSENTIA ORDER" and comply with the deadlines and requirements for filing. See subsection (d), below, Chapter 5.2 (Filing a Motion), Appendix E (Cover Pages. If the respondent is represented by a practitioner of record or has received document assistance from a practitioner, the motion must be accompanied by a Form EOIR-28 or Form EOIR-61. See Chapter 2.1 (Representation and Appearances Generally). To ensure that the immigration court has the respondent's current address, a change of address form (EOIR-33/IC) should be filed with the motion. A filing fee or fee waiver request may be required, depending on the nature of the motion. See 8 C.F.R. § 1003.24(b)(2).

(c) Deportation and Exclusion Proceedings — The standards for motions to reopen to rescind in absentia orders in deportation and exclusion proceedings differ from the standards in removal proceedings. See Chapter 7 (Other Proceedings before Immigration Judges). The provisions in subsection (d), below, apply to removal proceedings only. Parties in deportation or exclusion proceedings should carefully review the controlling law and regulations. See 8 C.F.R. § 1003.23(b)(4)(iii).

(d) Removal Proceedings — The following provisions apply to motions to reopen to rescind in absentia orders in removal proceedings only. Parties should note that, in removal proceedings, an in absentia order may be rescinded *only* upon the granting of a motion to reopen. The Board of Immigration Appeals does not have jurisdiction to consider direct appeals of in absentia orders in removal proceedings.

    (1) Content — A motion to reopen to rescind an in absentia order must demonstrate that:

- the failure to appear was because of exceptional circumstances;

- the failure to appear was because the respondent did not receive proper notice; or

- the failure to appear was because the respondent was in federal or state custody and the failure to appear was through no fault of the respondent.

INA § 240(b)(5)(C), 8 C.F.R. § 1003.23(b)(4)(ii). The term "exceptional circumstances" refers to exceptional circumstances beyond the control of the respondent (such as battery or extreme cruelty to the respondent or any child or parent of the respondent, serious illness of the respondent or serious illness or death of the spouse, child, or parent of the respondent, but not including less compelling circumstances). INA § 240(e)(1).

    (2) Time limits —

        (A) Within 180 days — If the motion to reopen to rescind an in absentia order is based on an allegation that the failure to appear was because of exceptional circumstances, the motion must be filed within 180 days after the in absentia order. See INA § 240(b)(5)(C), 8 C.F.R. § 1003.23(b)(4)(ii).

(B) At any time — If the motion to reopen to rescind an in absentia order is based on an allegation that the respondent did not receive proper notice of the hearing, or that the respondent was in federal or state custody and the failure to appear was through no fault of the respondent, the motion may be filed at any time. See INA § 240(b)(5)(C), 8 C.F.R. § 1003.23(b)(4)(ii).

(C) Responses — Responses to motions to reopen to rescind in absentia orders are due within ten (10) days after the motion was received by the immigration court, unless otherwise specified by the immigration judge.

(3) Number limits — The respondent is permitted to file only one motion to reopen to rescind an in absentia order. 8 C.F.R. § 1003.23(b)(4)(ii).

(4) Automatic stay — The removal of the respondent is automatically stayed pending disposition by the immigration judge of the motion to reopen to rescind an in absentia order in removal proceedings. See INA § 240(b)(5)(C), 8 C.F.R. § 1003.23(b)(4)(ii).

5.10   Other Motions

(a) Motion to Continue — A request for a continuance of any hearing should be made by written motion. Oral motions to continue are discouraged. The motion should set forth in detail the reasons for the request and, if appropriate, be supported by evidence. See Chapter 5.2(e) (Evidence). It should also include the date and time of the hearing, as well as preferred dates that the party is available to re-schedule the hearing. However, parties should be mindful that the immigration court retains discretion to schedule continued cases on dates that the court deems appropriate.

The motion should be filed with a cover page labeled "MOTION TO CONTINUE" and comply with the deadlines and requirements for filing. See Chapter 5.2 (Filing a Motion), Appendix E (Cover Pages).

The filing of a motion to continue does not excuse the appearance of a respondent or practitioner of record at any scheduled hearing. Therefore, until the motion is granted, parties must appear at all hearings as originally scheduled.

(b) Motion to Advance — A request to advance a hearing date (move the hearing to an earlier date) should be made by written motion. A motion to advance should completely articulate the reasons for the request. The motion should be filed with a cover page labeled "MOTION TO ADVANCE" and comply with the deadlines and requirements for filing. See Chapter 5.2 (Filing a Motion), Appendix E (Cover Pages).

(c) Motion to Change Venue — A request to change venue should be made by written motion. The motion should be supported by documentary evidence. See Chapter 5.2(e) (Evidence). The motion should contain the following information:

- the date and time of the next scheduled hearing

- a fixed street address where the respondent may be reached for further hearing notification

- if the address at which the respondent is receiving mail has changed, a properly completed change of address form (Form EOIR-33/IC)

- a detailed explanation of the reasons for the request

See generally *Matter of Rahman*, 20 I&N Dec. 480 (BIA 1992), 8 C.F.R. § 1003.20.

The motion should be filed with a cover page labeled "MOTION TO CHANGE VENUE," accompanied by a proposed order for change of venue and comply with the deadlines and requirements for filing. See Chapter 5.2 (Filing a Motion), Appendix E (Cover Pages). The motion should demonstrate good cause for the change in venue, and any grant or denial of such a motion is within the discretion of the immigration judge. 8 C.F.R. § 1003.20(b); *Matter of Rivera*, 19 I&N Dec. 688 (BIA 1988).

The filing of a motion to change venue does not excuse the appearance of a respondent or practitioner of record at any scheduled hearing. Therefore, until the motion is granted, parties must appear at all hearings as originally scheduled.

(d) Motion for Substitution of Counsel — See Chapter 2.1(b)(3) (Change in Representation).

(e) Motion to Withdraw as Counsel — See Chapter 2.3(b)(3) (Change in Representation).

(f) Motion for Extension — See Chapter 3.1(c)(4) (Motions for extensions of filing deadlines).

(g) Motion for Master Calendar Hearing — See Chapter 3.1(c)(5) (Motions for master calendar hearing).

(h) Motion to Accept an Untimely Filing — See Chapter 3.1(d)(2) (Untimely filings).

(i) Motion for Closed Hearing — See Chapter 4.9 (Public Access).

(j) Motion to Waive Practitioner of Record's Appearance — See Chapter 4.15 (Master Calendar Hearing).

(k) Motion to Waive Respondent's Appearance — See Chapter 4.15 (Master Calendar Hearing).

(l) Motion to Permit Telephonic Appearance — See Chapter 4.15 (Master Calendar Hearing).

(m) Motion to Request an Interpreter — See Chapter 4.15 (Master Calendar Hearing).

(n) Motion for Video Testimony — See Chapter 4.15 (Master Calendar Hearing).

(o) Motion to Present Telephonic Testimony — See Chapter 4.15 (Master Calendar Hearing).

(p) Motion for Subpoena — See Chapter 4.20 (Subpoenas).

(q) Motion for Consolidation — See Chapter 4.21 (Combining and Separating Cases).

(r) Motion for Severance — See Chapter 4.21 (Combining and Separating Cases).

(s) Motion to Stay Removal or Deportation — See Chapter 8 (Stays).

(t) Motions in Disciplinary Proceedings — Motions in proceedings involving the discipline of a practitioner are discussed in Chapter 10 (Discipline of Practitioners).

(u) Motion to Recalendar — When proceedings have been administratively closed and a party wishes to reopen the proceedings, the proper motion is a motion to recalendar, not a motion to reopen. A motion to recalendar should provide the date and the reason the case was closed. If available, a copy of the closure order should be attached to the motion. The motion should be filed with a cover page labeled "MOTION TO RECALENDAR" and comply with the requirements for filing. See Chapter 5.2 (Filing a Motion), Appendix E (Cover Pages). To ensure that the immigration court has the respondent's current address, a change of address form (EOIR-33/IC) should be filed with the motion. Motions to recalendar are not subject to time and number restrictions.

(v) Motion to Amend — The immigration judge entertains motions to amend previous filings in limited situations (e.g., to correct a clerical error in a filing). The motion should clearly articulate what needs to be corrected in the previous filing. The filing of a motion to amend does not affect any existing motion deadlines.

The motion should be filed with a cover page labeled "MOTION TO AMEND" and comply with the requirements for filing. See Chapter 5.2 (Filing a Motion), Appendix E (Cover Pages).

(w) Motion for Prima Facie Determination of Eligibility — Noncitizens with a pending application for suspension of deportation under section 244(a)(3) of the Act, or cancellation of removal under section 240A(b)(2) of the Act, may file a motion with the immigration court for a determination that they are a "qualified" noncitizen for purposes of receiving public benefits under section 431 of the Personal Responsibility and Work Opportunity Reconciliation Act of 1996 as a noncitizen who has demonstrated prima facie eligibility for such relief from removal.

In order to file a motion for prima facie determination, the noncitizen must have filed or is filing concurrently a completed application for suspension of deportation under section 244(a)(3) or cancellation of removal under section 240A(b)(2) of the INA. The motion must be accompanied by a signed statement by the noncitizen, under penalty of perjury, stating whether they have been convicted of any crime and, if so, any details about the offense(s). Any additional statements or evidence that the noncitizen wishes the Court to consider must also be attached to the motion.

Responses to motions for prima facie determination are due within five (5) business days after the motion was received by the immigration court, unless otherwise specified by the immigration judge.

Once an appeal is filed with the Board of Immigration Appeals, the immigration judge no longer has jurisdiction over the case. See Chapter 5.2(a) (Where to file). Thus, motions for prima facie determination should not be filed with the immigration court after an appeal is taken to the Board.

(x) Other Types of Motions — The immigration court entertains other types of motions as appropriate to the facts and law of each particular case, provided that the motion is timely, is properly filed, is clearly captioned, and complies with the general motion requirements. See Chapter 5.2 (Filing a Motion), Appendix E (Cover Pages).

5.11 Decisions

Immigration judges decide motions either orally at a hearing or in writing. If the decision is in writing, it will generally be served on the parties by regular mail or electronic notification in ECAS cases if both parties are participating.

5.12 Response to Motion

Responses to motions must comply with the deadlines and requirements for filing. See 8 C.F.R. § 1003.23(a), Chapter 3 (Filing with the Immigration Court). A motion is deemed unopposed unless timely response is made. Parties should note that unopposed motions are not necessarily granted. Immigration judges may deny a motion before the close of the response period without waiting for a response from the opposing party if the motion does not comply with the applicable legal requirements. Examples include:

- Denial of a motion to withdraw as counsel of record that does not contain a statement that the practitioner has notified the respondent of the request to withdraw as counsel or, if the respondent could not be notified, an explanation of the efforts made to notify the respondent of the request. See Chapter 2.1(b)(3)(C)) (Withdrawal of counsel).

- Denial of a motion to change venue that does not identify the fixed address where the respondent may be reached for further hearing notification. See Chapter 5.10(c) (Motion to Change Venue), 8 C.F.R. § 1003.20(b).

This page intentionally left blank.

Chapter 6 Appeals of Immigration Judge Decisions

6.1   Appeals Generally

The Board of Immigration Appeals has nationwide jurisdiction to review decisions of immigration judges. See 8 C.F.R. § 1003.1, Chapter 1.2(c) (Relationship to the Board of Immigration Appeals). Accordingly, appeals of immigration judge decisions should be made to the Board. Appeals of immigration judge decisions are distinct from motions to reopen or motions to reconsider, which are filed with the immigration court following a decision ending proceedings. See Chapter 5 (Motions before the Immigration Court).

This chapter is limited to appeals from the decisions of immigration judges in removal, deportation, and exclusion proceedings. Other kinds of appeals are discussed in the following chapters:

Chapter 7   Other Proceedings before Immigration Judges

Chapter 9   Detention and Bond

Chapter 10   Discipline of Practitioners

For detailed guidance on appeals, parties should consult the Board of Immigration Appeals Practice Manual.

6.2   Process

(a) Who May Appeal — An immigration judge's decision may be appealed only by the respondent subject to the proceeding, the respondent's practitioner of record, or the Department of Homeland Security. See 8 C.F.R. § 1003.3.

(b) How to Appeal — To appeal an immigration judge's decision, a party must file a properly completed and executed Notice of Appeal (Form EOIR-26) with the Board of Immigration Appeals. The Form EOIR-26 must be received by the Board no later than 30 calendar days after the immigration judge renders an oral decision or mails or sends electronic notification of a written decision. See 8 C.F.R. § 1003.38. Parties must comply with all instructions on the Form EOIR-26.

Appeals are subject to strict requirements. For detailed information on these requirements, parties should consult the Board of Immigration Appeals Practice Manual.

6.3   Jurisdiction

After an appeal has been filed, jurisdiction shifts between the immigration court and the Board of Immigration Appeals depending on the nature and status of the appeal. For detailed guidance on whether the immigration court or the Board has jurisdiction over a particular matter in which an appeal has been filed, parties should consult the Board of Immigration Appeals Practice Manual. See Appendix J (Filing Motions).

6.4   Waiver of Appeal

(a) Effect of Appeal Waiver — If the opportunity to appeal is knowingly and voluntarily waived, the decision of the immigration judge becomes final. See 8 C.F.R. § 1003.39. If a party waives appeal at the conclusion of proceedings before the immigration judge, that party generally may not file an appeal thereafter. See 8 C.F.R. § 1003.3(a)(1); *Matter of Shih*, 20 I&N Dec. 697 (BIA 1993). See also 8 C.F.R. § 1003.1(d)(2)(i)(G).

(b) Challenging a Waiver of Appeal — Generally, a party who waives appeal cannot retract, withdraw, or otherwise undo that waiver. If a party wishes to challenge the validity of their waiver of appeal, the party may do so in one of two ways: either in a timely motion filed with the immigration judge that explains why the appeal waiver was not valid *or* in an appeal filed directly with the Board of Immigration Appeals that explains why the appeal waiver was not valid. *Matter of Patino*, 23 I&N Dec. 74 (BIA 2001). Once an appeal is filed, jurisdiction vests with the Board, and the motion can no longer be ruled upon by the immigration judge. For detailed guidance on whether the immigration court or the Board has jurisdiction over a particular matter in which an appeal has been filed, parties should consult the Board of Immigration Appeals Practice Manual.

6.5   Certification

An immigration judge may ask the Board of Immigration Appeals to review their decision. See 8 C.F.R. §§ 1003.1(c), 1003.7. This is known as "certifying" the case to the Board. When a case is certified, an immigration court serves a notice of certification on the parties. Generally, a briefing schedule is served on the parties following certification.

The certification of a case is separate from any appeal in the case. Therefore, a party wishing to appeal must file an appeal *even if* the immigration judge has certified the case to the Board. See 8 C.F.R. § 1003.3(d).

6.6   Additional Information

For detailed guidance on appeals, parties should consult the Board of Immigration Appeals Practice Manual, which is available on the EOIR website.

Chapter 7 Other Proceedings before Immigration Judges

7.1   Overview

While the vast majority of proceedings conducted by immigration judges are removal proceedings, immigration judges have jurisdiction over other kinds of proceedings as well. This chapter provides a brief overview of these other kinds of proceedings. They include:

- deportation proceedings and exclusion proceedings

- rescission proceedings

- limited proceedings, including:

    o credible fear proceedings

    o reasonable fear proceedings

    o claimed status review

    o asylum-only proceedings

    o withholding-only proceedings

- streamlined removal proceedings

Removal proceedings are discussed in Chapter 4 (Hearings before the Immigration Judges). Additional proceedings conducted by immigration judges are discussed in the following chapters:

Chapter 9   Detention and Bond

Chapter 10   Discipline of Practitioners

7.2   Deportation Proceedings and Exclusion Proceedings

(a) In General —

(1) Replaced by removal proceedings — Beginning with proceedings commenced on April 1, 1997, deportation and exclusion proceedings have been replaced by removal proceedings. See generally INA §§ 239, 240, 8 C.F.R. §§ 1003.12 et seq., 1240.1 et seq. However, immigration judges continue to conduct deportation and exclusion proceedings in certain cases that began before April 1, 1997.

(2) Compared with removal proceedings — The procedures in deportation and exclusion proceedings are generally similar to the procedures in removal proceedings. See Chapters 2 (Appearances before the Immigration Court), 3 (Filing with the Immigration Court), 4 (Hearings before the Immigration Judges), 5 (Motions before the Immigration Court), 6 (Appeals of Immigration Judge Decisions). However, deportation and exclusion proceedings are significantly different from removal proceedings in areas such as burden of proof, forms of relief available, and custody. Accordingly, parties in deportation and exclusion proceedings should carefully review the laws and regulations pertaining to those proceedings. The information in this chapter is provided as a general guideline only.

(b) Deportation Proceedings —

(1) Order to Show Cause — Deportation proceedings began when the former Immigration and Naturalization Service (INS) filed an Order to Show Cause (Form I-221) with the immigration court after serving it on the respondent in person or by certified mail. See former INA § 242B(a)(1), 8 C.F.R. § 1240.40 et seq. See also Chapter 1.2 (Function of the Office of the Chief Immigration Judge). Similar to a Notice to Appear (Form I-862), an Order to Show Cause (Form I-221) is a written notice containing factual allegations and charge(s) of deportability.

(2) Hearing notification — In deportation proceedings, hearing notices from the immigration court are served on the parties, personally or by certified mail, at least 14 days prior to the hearing.

(3) Grounds of deportability — The grounds for deportation that apply in deportation proceedings are listed in former INA § 241. In some cases, those grounds are different from the grounds of deportability in removal proceedings. Compare former INA § 241 (prior to 1997) with current INA § 237.

(4) Forms of relief — For the most part, the same forms of relief are available in deportation proceedings as in removal proceedings. However, there are important differences. Parties in deportation proceedings should carefully review the relevant law and regulations.

(5) Appeals — In most cases, an immigration judge's decision in a deportation proceeding can be appealed to the Board of Immigration Appeals. See Chapter 6 (Appeals of Immigration Judge Decisions).

(c) Exclusion Proceedings —

(1) Notice to Applicant Detained for Hearing — Exclusion proceedings began when the Immigration and Naturalization Service (INS) filed a Notice to Applicant for Admission Detained for Hearing before an Immigration Judge (Form I-122). See former INA § 242(b), 8 C.F.R. § 1240.30 et seq. The Form I-122 is a written notice containing the charge(s) of excludability. Unlike the Order to Show Cause, the Form I-122 *does not* contain factual allegations.

(2) Hearing notification — In exclusion proceedings, the noncitizen must be given a reasonable opportunity to be present at the hearing. Note that, in exclusion proceedings, notice to the noncitizen is not governed by the same standards as in deportation proceedings. See *Matter of Nafi*, 19 I&N Dec. 430 (BIA 1987).

(3) Closed to public — Exclusion hearings are closed to the public unless the applicant requests that the public be allowed to attend.

(4) Grounds of excludability — The grounds for exclusion are listed in the former INA § 212. In some cases, the grounds of excludability in exclusion proceedings are different from the grounds of inadmissibility in removal proceedings. Compare former INA § 212 (prior to 1997) with current INA § 212.

(5) Forms of relief — For the most part, the same forms of relief are available in exclusion proceedings as in removal proceedings. However, there are important differences. Parties in exclusion proceedings should carefully review the relevant law and regulations.

(6) Appeals — An immigration judge's decision in an exclusion proceeding can be appealed to the Board of Immigration Appeals. See Chapter 6 (Appeals of Immigration Judge Decisions).

7.3   Rescission Proceedings

(a) In General — In a rescission proceeding, an immigration judge determines whether a noncitizen's status as a lawful permanent resident should be "rescinded," or taken away, because the noncitizen was not entitled to become a lawful permanent resident. See generally 8 C.F.R. § 1246.1 et seq. A noncitizen's lawful permanent resident status may not be rescinded if more than 5 years have passed since the noncitizen became a lawful permanent resident. See INA § 246(a).

(b) Notice of Intent to Rescind — A rescission proceeding begins when the Department of Homeland Security personally serves a noncitizen with a Notice of Intent to Rescind. The noncitizen has 30 days to submit a sworn answer in writing and/or request a hearing before an immigration judge. A rescission hearing is held if the noncitizen files a timely answer which contests or denies any allegation in the Notice of Intent to Rescind *or* the noncitizen requests a hearing.

(c) Conduct of Hearing — Rescission proceedings are conducted in a manner similar to removal proceedings. See Chapter 4 (Hearings before the Immigration Judges).

(d) Appeal — An immigration judge's decision in a rescission proceeding can be appealed to the Board of Immigration Appeals.

7.4   Limited Proceedings

(a) In General — Certain noncitizens can be removed from the United States without being placed into removal proceedings. However, in some circumstances, these individuals may be afforded limited proceedings, including credible fear review, reasonable fear review, claimed status review, asylum-only proceedings, and withholding-only proceedings.

(b) Classes of Noncitizens — The following noncitizens can be removed from the United States without being placed into removal proceedings. These noncitizens are afforded limited proceedings as described below.

(1) Expedited removal under INA § 235(b)(1) — The following noncitizens are subject to "expedited removal" under INA § 235(b)(1):

- noncitizens arriving at a port of entry without valid identity or travel documents, as required, or with fraudulent documents

- noncitizens interdicted at sea (in international or U.S. waters) and brought to the United States

- individuals who have not been admitted or paroled into the United States and who have been continuously present in the United States for fewer than 14 days

- individuals paroled into the United States after April 1, 1997, and whose parole has since been terminated

(A) Exceptions — The following noncitizens are *not* subject to expedited removal under INA § 235(b)(1):

- lawful permanent residents

- noncitizens granted refugee or asylee status

- noncitizens seeking asylum while applying for admission under the visa waiver program

- minors, unless they have committed certain crimes

(B) Limited proceedings afforded — As described below, noncitizens subject to expedited removal under INA § 235(b)(1) are afforded the following proceedings:

- if the noncitizen expresses a fear of persecution or torture, the noncitizen is placed into "credible fear proceedings," as described in subsection (d), (below)

- if the individual claims to be a United States citizen or a lawful permanent resident, or that they have been granted refugee or asylee status, the individual is allowed a "claimed status review," as described in subsection (f), (below)

(2) Expedited removal under INA § 238(b) — Noncitizens who are not lawful permanent residents and who have been convicted of aggravated felonies are subject to "expedited removal" under INA § 238(b). If such a noncitizen expresses a fear of persecution or torture, the noncitizen is placed into "reasonable fear proceedings." See subsection (e), below.

(3) Reinstatement of prior orders under INA § 241(a)(5) — Under INA § 241(a)(5), noncitizens who are subject to reinstatement of prior orders of removal are not entitled to removal proceedings. If such a noncitizen expresses a fear of persecution or torture, the noncitizen is placed into "reasonable fear proceedings." See subsection (e), below.

(4) Stowaways — If a stowaway expresses a fear of persecution or torture, they are placed into credible fear proceedings. See INA § 235(a)(2), subsection (d), below.

(5) Others — In certain circumstances, the noncitizens listed below may be placed into asylum-only proceedings. See subsection (g), below.

- stowaways with a credible fear of persecution or torture

- crewmembers (D visa applicants)

- certain cooperating witnesses and informants (S visa applicants)

- visa waiver applicants and visa waiver overstays

- noncitizens subject to removal under INA § 235(c) on security grounds

(c) Custody in Limited Proceedings — A noncitizen subject to limited proceedings may be detained during the proceedings. Immigration judges have no jurisdiction over custody decisions for these noncitizens.

(d) Credible Fear Proceedings — Credible fear proceedings involve stowaways and noncitizens subject to expedited removal under INA § 235(b)(1). See subsections (b)(1), (b)(4), above. If such a noncitizen expresses a fear of persecution or torture to the Department of Homeland Security (DHS) immigration officer upon being detained by DHS or applying to enter the United States, then the noncitizen is interviewed by a United States Citizenship and Immigration Services (USCIS) asylum officer who evaluates whether the noncitizen possesses a credible fear of persecution or torture. See generally INA § 235(b)(1)(B).

(1) Credible fear standard — "Credible fear of persecution" means that there is a significant possibility that the noncitizen can establish eligibility for asylum under INA § 208 or withholding of removal ("restriction on removal") under INA § 241(b)(3). The credibility of the noncitizen's statements in support of the claim, and other facts known to the reviewing official, are taken into account. 8 C.F.R. §§ 208.30(e)(2), 1003.42(d).

"Credible fear of torture" means there is a significant possibility that the noncitizen is eligible for withholding of removal ("restriction on removal") or deferral of removal under the Convention Against Torture pursuant to 8 C.F.R. §§ 208.16 or 208.17. 8 C.F.R. §§ 208.30(e)(3), 1003.42(d).

(2) If the USCIS asylum officer finds credible fear —

(A) Stowaways — If the USCIS asylum officer finds that a stowaway has a credible fear of persecution or torture, the stowaway is placed in asylum-only proceedings before an immigration judge. See 8 C.F.R. § 208.30(f). In asylum-only proceedings, the stowaway can apply for asylum, withholding of removal ("restriction on removal") under INA § 241(b)(3), and protection under the Convention Against Torture. See subsection (g), below.

(B) Noncitizens subject to expedited removal under INA § 235(b)(1) — If the USCIS asylum officer finds that a noncitizen subject to expedited removal under INA § 235(b)(1) has a credible fear of persecution or torture, USCIS may, at its discretion, conduct further proceedings to evaluate the noncitizen's eligibility for asylum. If USCIS does so, the written record of the noncitizen's positive credible fear finding is deemed by USCIS to be an application for asylum. USCIS schedules an asylum merits interview for the noncitizen with an asylum officer and, following the interview, decides whether to grant the noncitizen's asylum application. If USCIS decides not to grant the asylum application, the noncitizen is placed into streamlined removal proceedings, as described further in Chapter 7.6. See 8 C.F.R. §§ 208.3(a)(2), 208.14(c)(1), 208.30(f), 1240.17.

If—subsequent to a credible fear finding—USCIS chooses not to consider the noncitizen's eligibility for asylum further, then USCIS will place the noncitizen in removal proceedings before an immigration judge. See 8 C.F.R. § 208.30(f). In removal proceedings, the noncitizen has the same rights, obligations, and opportunities for relief as any other noncitizen in removal proceedings. See Chapter 4 (Hearings before the Immigration Judges).

(3) If the USCIS asylum officer does not find credible fear — If the USCIS asylum officer finds that the noncitizen does *not* have a credible fear of persecution or torture, the noncitizen may request that an immigration judge review this finding. See 8 C.F.R. § 208.30(g).

(4) Credible fear review by an immigration judge — The credible fear review is conducted according to the provisions in (A) through (I), below. See generally INA § 235(b)(1)(B), 8 C.F.R. § 1003.42.

(A) Timing — The credible fear review must be concluded no later than 7 days after the date of the USCIS asylum officer's decision. If possible, the credible fear review should be concluded 24 hours after the decision. 8 C.F.R. § 1003.42(e).

(B) Location — If possible, the credible fear review is conducted in person. However, because of the time constraints, the credible fear review may be conducted by video or telephone conference. 8 C.F.R. § 1003.42(c); see Chapter 4.7 (Hearings by Video or Telephone Conference).

(C) Representation — Prior to the credible fear review, the noncitizen may consult with a person or persons of the noncitizen's choosing. 8 C.F.R. § 1003.42(c). In the discretion of the immigration judge, persons consulted may be present during the credible fear review. However, the noncitizen is not represented at the credible fear review. Accordingly, persons acting on the noncitizen's behalf are not entitled to make opening statements, call and question witnesses, conduct cross examinations, object to evidence, or make closing arguments.

(D) Record of Proceedings — DHS must give the complete record of the USCIS asylum officer's credible fear determination to the immigration court. This record includes any notes taken by the USCIS asylum officer. The immigration judge creates a record, which is kept separate from the Record of Proceedings in any subsequent immigration court proceeding involving the noncitizens.

(E) Conduct of hearing — A credible fear review is not as exhaustive or in-depth as an asylum hearing in removal proceedings. Rather, a credible fear review is simply a review of the USCIS asylum officer's decision. Either the noncitizen or DHS may introduce oral or written statements, and the court provides an interpreter if necessary. Evidence may be introduced at the discretion of the immigration judge. The hearing is recorded. Parties should be mindful that all requests for continuances are subject to the statutory time limits. See (A), above.

(5) If the immigration judge finds credible fear —

(A) Stowaways — If the immigration judge finds that a stowaway has a credible fear of persecution or torture, the stowaway is placed in asylum-only proceedings. See 8 C.F.R. § 1208.30(g)(2)(iv)(C). In asylum-only proceedings, the stowaway can apply for asylum, withholding of removal ("restriction on removal") under INA § 241(b)(3), and protection under the Convention Against Torture. See subsection (g), below.

(B) Noncitizens subject to expedited removal under INA § 235(b)(1) — If the immigration judge finds that a noncitizen subject to expedited removal under INA § 235(b)(1) has a credible fear of persecution or torture, USCIS may, in its discretion, conduct further proceedings to consider the noncitizen's eligibility for asylum. If USCIS does so, it deems the written record of the noncitizen's positive credible fear finding as an application for asylum. USCIS then schedules an asylum merits interview for the noncitizen with an asylum officer and, following the interview, decides whether to grant the noncitizen's asylum application. If USCIS decides not to grant the asylum application, the noncitizen is placed into streamlined removal proceedings, as described in Chapter 7.6 (Streamlined Removal Proceedings). See 8 C.F.R. §§ 208.3(a)(2), 208.14(c)(1), 1208.30(f), 1240.17.

If—subsequent to a credible fear finding—USCIS chooses not to consider the noncitizen's eligibility for asylum further, then USCIS will place the noncitizen in removal proceedings. See 8 C.F.R. §§ 1003.42(f), 1208.30(g)(2)(iv)(B). In removal proceedings, the noncitizen has the same rights, obligations, and opportunities for relief, including the opportunity to apply for asylum, as any other noncitizen in removal proceedings. See Chapter 4 (Hearings before the Immigration Judges).

(6) If the immigration judge does not find credible fear — If the immigration judge does not find credible fear of persecution or torture, the noncitizen is returned to DHS for removal. Neither party may appeal an immigration judge's ruling in a credible fear review. However, after providing notice to the immigration judge, DHS may reconsider its determination that a noncitizen does not have a credible fear of persecution. See 8 C.F.R. § 1208.30(g)(2)(iv)(A).

(e) Reasonable Fear Proceedings — Reasonable fear proceedings involve noncitizens subject to expedited removal under INA § 238(b) and noncitizens subject to reinstatement of prior orders of removal under INA § 241(a)(5). See subsections (b)(2), (b)(3), above. If such a noncitizen expresses a fear of persecution or torture to the Department of Homeland Security (DHS) immigration officer, the noncitizen is interviewed by a DHS asylum officer who evaluates whether the noncitizen has a "reasonable fear of persecution or torture." See generally 8 C.F.R. § 1208.31.

(1) Reasonable fear standard — "Reasonable fear of persecution or torture" means a reasonable possibility that the noncitizen would be persecuted on account of their race, religion, nationality, membership in a particular social group, or political opinion, or a reasonable possibility that the noncitizen would be tortured if returned to the country of removal. The bars to eligibility for withholding of removal ("restriction on removal") under INA § 241(b)(3)(B) are not considered. 8 C.F.R. § 1208.31(c).

(2) If the USCIS asylum officer finds reasonable fear — If the USCIS asylum officer finds that the noncitizen has a reasonable fear of persecution or torture, the noncitizen is placed in withholding-only proceedings before an immigration judge. See 8 C.F.R. § 208.31(e). In withholding-only proceedings, the noncitizen can apply for withholding of removal ("restriction on removal") under INA § 241(b)(3) and protection under the Convention Against Torture. See subsection (h), below.

(3) If the USCIS asylum officer does not find reasonable fear — If the USCIS asylum officer finds that the noncitizen does not have a reasonable fear of persecution or torture, the noncitizen may request that an immigration judge review this finding. See 8 C.F.R. § 208.31(f).

(4) Reasonable fear review by an immigration judge — The reasonable fear review is conducted according to the provisions in (A) through (E), below. See generally 8 C.F.R. § 1208.31.

(A) Timing — In the absence of exceptional circumstances, the reasonable fear review is conducted within 10 days after the case is referred to the immigration court. 8 C.F.R. § 1208.31(g) .

(B) Location — If possible, the reasonable fear review is conducted in person. However, because of the time constraints, the reasonable fear review may be conducted by video or telephone conference. See Chapter 4.7 (Hearings by Video or Telephone Conference).

(C) Representation — Subject to the immigration judge's discretion, the noncitizen may be represented by a practitioner of record during the reasonable fear review at no expense to the government. 8 C.F.R. § 1208.31(c) .

(D) Record of Proceedings — DHS must file the complete record of the USCIS asylum officer's reasonable fear determination with the immigration court. This record includes any notes taken by the USCIS asylum officer. 8 C.F.R. § 1208.31(g) The immigration judge creates a record, which is kept separate from the Record of Proceedings in any subsequent immigration court proceeding involving the noncitizen.

(E) Conduct of hearing — A reasonable fear review hearing is not as comprehensive or in-depth as a withholding of removal hearing in removal proceedings. Rather, it is a review of the USCIS asylum officer's decision. Either party may introduce oral or written statements, and the court provides an interpreter if necessary. Evidence may be introduced at the discretion of the immigration judge. The hearing is recorded. Parties should be mindful that all requests for continuances are subject to the statutory time limits. See (A), above.

(5) If the immigration judge finds reasonable fear — If the immigration judge finds that the noncitizen has a reasonable fear of persecution or torture, the noncitizen is placed in withholding-only proceedings. See 8 C.F.R. § 1208.31(g)(2). In withholding-only proceedings, the noncitizen can apply for withholding of removal ("A restriction on removal") under INA § 241(b)(3) and protection under the Convention Against Torture. See subsection (h).

(6) If the immigration judge does not find reasonable fear — If the immigration judge does not find a reasonable fear of persecution or torture, the noncitizen is returned to DHS for removal. There is no appeal from an immigration judge's ruling in a reasonable fear review. See 8 C.F.R. § 1208.31(g)(1).

(f) Claimed Status Review — If an individual is found by a Department of Homeland Security (DHS) immigration officer to be subject to expedited removal under INA § 235(b)(1), but claims to be a United States citizen or lawful permanent resident, or to have been granted asylum or admitted to the United States as a refugee, the DHS immigration officer will attempt to verify that claim. If the claim cannot be verified, the individual is allowed to make a statement under oath. The case is then reviewed by an immigration judge in a "claimed status review." See generally 8 C.F.R. § 1235.3(b)(5).

(1) Timing — Claimed status reviews are scheduled as expeditiously as possible, preferably no later than 7 days after the case was referred to the immigration court and, if possible, within 24 hours. Claims to United States citizenship may require more time to permit the noncitizen to obtain relevant documentation.

(2) Location — If possible, the claimed status review is conducted in person. However, because of the time constraints, the claimed status review may be conducted by video or telephone conference. See Chapter 4.7 (Hearings by Video or Telephone Conference).

(3) Representation — Prior to the claimed status review, the individual subject to the review may consult with a person or persons of their choosing. In the discretion of the immigration judge, persons consulted may be present during the claimed status review. However, the individual subject to the review is not represented during the review. Accordingly, persons acting on their behalf are not entitled to make opening statements, call and question witnesses, conduct cross examinations, object to evidence, or make closing arguments.

(4) Record of Proceedings — The immigration judge creates a Record of Proceedings. If an individual subject to a claimed status review is later placed in removal proceedings, the Record of Proceedings for the claimed status review is merged with the Record of Proceedings for the removal proceedings.

(5) Conduct of hearing — Either party may introduce oral or written statements, and an interpreter is provided if necessary. Though the claimed status review is limited in nature, claims to status, particularly claims to United States citizenship, can be complicated and may require extensive evidence. Therefore, the immigration judge has the discretion to continue proceedings to allow DHS and the person making the claim to collect and submit evidence. The hearing is recorded.

(6) If the immigration judge verifies the claimed status — If the immigration judge determines that the individual subject to the review is a United States citizen or lawful permanent resident, or that they have been granted asylum or refugee status, the expedited removal order is vacated, or cancelled, and the proceedings are terminated.

Unless the immigration judge determines that the person in proceedings is a United States citizen, DHS may elect to place them in removal proceedings. In removal proceedings, the individual has the same rights, obligations, and opportunities for relief as any other noncitizen in removal proceedings. See Chapter 4 (Hearings before the Immigration Judges).

(7) If the immigration judge cannot verify the claimed status — If the immigration judge determines that the subject of a claimed status review is not a United States citizen or lawful permanent resident, and that they have not been granted asylee or refugee status, the individual is returned to DHS for removal. There is no appeal from an immigration judge's ruling in a claimed status review.

(g) Asylum-Only Proceedings — Asylum-only proceedings are limited proceedings in which the immigration judge considers applications for asylum, withholding of removal ("restriction on removal") under INA § 241(b)(3), and protection under the Convention Against Torture.

(1) Beginning asylum-only proceedings — Asylum-only proceedings are commenced as follows, depending upon the status of the noncitizen.

(A) Stowaways with a credible fear of persecution or torture — When a USCIS asylum officer or an immigration judge finds that a stowaway has a credible fear of persecution or torture, the stowaway's matter is referred to the immigration court for an asylum-only proceeding. See 8 C.F.R. §§ 208.30(f), 1208.30(g)(2)(iv)(C).

(B) Crewmembers (D visa applicants) — When a noncitizen crewmember expresses a fear of persecution or torture to a DHS immigration officer, they are removed from the vessel and taken into DHS custody. The crewmember is then provided an Application for Asylum and for Withholding of Removal (Form I-589), which must be completed and returned to DHS within 10 days unless DHS extends the deadline for good cause. The application is then referred to the immigration court for an asylum-only proceeding. See 8 C.F.R. §§ 1208.2(c)(1)(i), 1208.5(b)(1)(ii).

(C) Visa waiver applicants and overstays — When a noncitizen who has applied for admission, been admitted, or overstayed their admission under the visa waiver program expresses a fear of persecution or torture to a DHS immigration officer, or applies for asylum with DHS, the matter may be referred to the immigration court for an asylum-only proceeding. See 8 C.F.R. §§ 1208.2(c)(1)(iii), 1208.2(c)(1)(iv).

(D) Certain cooperating witnesses and informants (S visa applicants) — When a noncitizen who has applied for admission, or been admitted, with an S visa expresses a fear of persecution or torture to a DHS immigration officer, or applies for asylum with DHS, the matter is referred to the immigration court for an asylum-only proceeding. See 8 C.F.R. § 1208.2(c)(1)(vi).

(E) Persons subject to removal under INA § 235(c) on security grounds — When a DHS immigration officer or an immigration judge suspects that an arriving noncitizen appears removable as described in INA § 235(c), the noncitizen is ordered removed, and the matter is referred to a DHS district director. A DHS regional director may then order the case referred to an immigration judge for an asylum-only proceeding. See 8 C.F.R. §§ 1208.2(c)(1)(v), 1235.8.

(2) Scope of the proceedings — Asylum-only proceedings are limited to applications for asylum, withholding of removal ("restriction on removal") under INA § 241(b)(3), and protection under the Convention Against Torture. Neither the noncitizen nor DHS may raise any other issues, including issues of admissibility, deportability, eligibility for waivers, and eligibility for any other form of relief. See 8 C.F.R. § 1208.2(c)(3)(i).

(3) Conduct of the proceedings — Asylum-only proceedings are conducted under the procedures governing removal proceedings. See 8 C.F.R. § 1208.2(c)(3). See also Chapter 4 (Hearings before the Immigration Judges).

(4) Appeals — Decisions by immigration judges in asylum-only proceedings may be appealed to the Board of Immigration Appeals.

(h) Withholding-Only Proceedings — Withholding-only proceedings are limited proceedings involving noncitizens subject to expedited removal under INA § 238(b) and noncitizens subject to reinstatement of prior orders of removal under INA § 241(a)(5), who have a reasonable fear of persecution or torture. See 8 C.F.R. § 1208.2(c)(2). In withholding-only proceedings, the immigration judge considers applications for withholding of removal ("restriction on removal") under INA § 241(b)(3) and protection under the Convention Against Torture.

(1) Beginning withholding-only proceedings — When a DHS asylum officer or immigration judge finds that a noncitizen subject to expedited removal under INA § 238(b) or a noncitizen subject to reinstatement of a prior order of removal under INA § 241(a)(5) has a reasonable fear of persecution or torture, the matter is referred to the immigration court for a withholding-only proceeding. See 8 C.F.R. §§ 208.31(e), 1208.31(g)(2).

(2) Scope of the proceedings — Withholding-only proceedings are limited to applications for withholding of removal ("restriction on removal") under INA § 241(b)(3) and protection under the Convention Against Torture. Neither the noncitizen nor DHS may raise any other issues, including issues of admissibility, deportability, eligibility for waivers, and eligibility for any other form of relief. 8 C.F.R. § 1208.2(c)(3)(i).

(3) Conduct of the proceedings — Withholding-only proceedings are conducted under the procedures governing removal proceedings. See 8 C.F.R. § 1208.2(c)(3). See also Chapter 4 (Hearings before the Immigration Judges).

(4) Appeals — Decisions by immigration judges in withholding-only proceedings may be appealed to the Board of Immigration Appeals.

7.5   ABC Settlement

(a) ABC Class Members — Members of the class covered by the ABC Settlement Agreement, who timely registered to receive benefits under the agreement (either by applying directly or by applying for TPS, if Salvadoran) may be entitled to certain rights and benefits pursuant to the agreement. See *American Baptist Churches v. Thornburgh*, 760 F. Supp. 796 (N.D. Cal. 1991). ABC class members include Salvadorans who entered the United States on or before September 19, 1990, and Guatemalans who entered the United States on or before October 1, 1990.[1]

---

[1] Administrative closure was expressly authorized for certain ABC class members in order to implement the ABC settlement agreement and provide such class members the opportunity to exercise their rights under the agreement. See 8 C.F.R. §§ 1240.62(b) and 1240.70(f)-(h); *ABC*, 760 F. Supp. at 805.

(b) Certain El Salvador and Guatemala Nationals — Section 203 of the Nicaraguan Adjustment and Central American Relief Act ("NACARA") provides that certain nationals of El Salvador and Guatemala are eligible to apply for suspension of deportation, or NACARA cancellation, under standards similar to those in effect prior to the enactment of the Illegal Immigration Reform and Immigrant Responsibility Act ("IIRIRA"). Pub. L. No. 105-100, 111 Stat. 2160 (1997).

To qualify for NACARA relief as a Salvadoran or Guatemalan national, the applicant must have either:

(1) filed an application for asylum on or before April 1, 1990; or

(2) registered for benefits under *American Baptist Churches v. Thornburgh*, 760 F. Supp. 796 (N.D. Cal. 1991) and not been apprehended at the time of entry if such entry occurred after December 19, 1990. 8 C.F.R. § 1240.61(a)(1)-(2).

A Salvadoran national is considered to have registered for *ABC* benefits if they entered the United States on or before September 19, 1990, and either applied for temporary protected status on or before October 31, 1991, or submitted an ABC registration form on or before October 31, 1991. 8 C.F.R. § 1240.60(1). A Guatemalan national is considered to have registered for *ABC* benefits if they entered the United States on or before October 1, 1990, and submitted an ABC registration form on or before December 31, 1991. 8 C.F.R. § 1240.60(2).

7.6   Streamlined Removal Proceedings

A noncitizen is placed into streamlined removal proceedings where the noncitizen was found to have a credible fear of persecution or torture and a USCIS asylum officer adjudicated but did not grant the noncitizen's application for asylum. If the noncitizen's spouse or child was included on the application, then the spouse or child is placed into streamlined removal proceedings as well.

Streamlined removal proceedings are conducted on a specific timeline and are subject to specific procedures, as discussed below. See generally 8 C.F.R. § 1240.17 (setting forth the timeline and procedural requirements of streamlined removal proceedings). Otherwise, streamlined removal proceedings are conducted under the same procedures as ordinary removal proceedings. See Chapter 4 (Hearings before the Immigration Judges).

(a) Initiation of Proceedings — Streamlined removal proceedings begin when DHS files a Notice to Appear (NTA) with the immigration court and serves it on the noncitizen. The NTA is annotated to reflect that the noncitizen is being placed in streamlined removal proceedings.

DHS will also, no later than the first master calendar hearing, serve the respondent and the immigration court with the record initiating proceedings. This is comprised of the written record of the positive credible fear finding, all unclassified information the asylum officer considered in adjudicating the respondent's applications, the transcript of the asylum merits interview, the asylum officer's written decision, and the Form I-213, *Record of Deportable/Inadmissible Alien*, pertaining to the respondent. See 8 C.F.R. §§ 208.9(f), 1240.17(c).

(b) Applications — In streamlined removal proceedings, the respondent is not required to file an Application for Asylum and for Withholding of Removal (Form I-589) with the immigration court. Instead, the written record of the positive credible fear determination is deemed an application for asylum, withholding of removal ("restriction on removal") under INA § 241(b)(3), and protection under the Convention Against Torture. See 8 C.F.R. § 1208.3(a)(2).

Respondents in streamlined removal proceedings may apply for any form of relief or protection from removal for which they may be eligible, including voluntary departure.

(c) Timeline of Proceedings —

    (1) Master calendar hearing — The initial master calendar hearing for cases subject to streamlined removal proceedings will be held between 30 and 35 days after the date DHS serves the NTA. See 8 C.F.R. § 1240.17(b).

    (2) Status conference — A status conference will be held between 30 and 35 days after the master calendar hearing. The purpose of the status conference is to take pleadings, identify and narrow the issues, determine whether the case can be decided on the documentary record, and, if necessary, prepare the case for a merits hearing. See 8 C.F.R. § 1240.17(f)(1), (2).

    (3) Merits hearing — In instances where the immigration judge has determined that a merits hearing is necessary, that hearing will be held between 60 and 65 days after the master calendar hearing. See 8 C.F.R. § 1240.17(f)(2).

(d) Continuances & Filing Extensions — In streamlined removal proceedings, the immigration judge may grant continuances and extend filing deadlines upon either party's motion. The standard for granting a continuance or extending a deadline depends on which party made the request and other factors. In addition, an immigration judge may continue a case, or extend a finding deadline, because of exigent circumstances, such as when the immigration judge, the respondent, or a practitioner of record is unavailable due to illness. See 8 C.F.R. § 1240.17(h)(4).

(e) Appeals — In streamlined removal proceedings, the respondent may appeal the immigration judge's decision to the Board of Immigration Appeals. See Chapter 6 (Appeals of Immigration Judge Decisions). DHS also may appeal an immigration judge's decision to the Board subject to limited exceptions. See 8 C.F.R. § 1240.17(i)(2).

(f) Other Provisions — Special provisions govern immigration judges' in absentia orders in streamlined removal proceedings. See 8 C.F.R. § 1240.17(d). In addition, some of the regulations' streamlining provisions do not apply in certain, specified situations. See 8 C.F.R. § 1240.17(k).

Chapter 8 Stays

8.1   In General

A stay prevents the Department of Homeland Security (DHS) from executing an order of removal, deportation, or exclusion. Stays are automatic in some instances and discretionary in others. This chapter provides general guidance regarding the procedures to follow when filing for a stay before the immigration court or the Board of Immigration Appeals (BIA). For particular cases, parties should note that the procedures are not the same before the immigration court and the BIA and should consult the controlling law and regulations. See INA §§ 240(b)(5)(C), 240(c)(7)(C)(iv); 8 C.F.R. §§ 1003.2(f), 1003.6, 1003.23(b)(1)(v), and 1003.23(b)(4)(ii), (iii)(C).

A noncitizen under a final order of deportation or removal may seek a stay of deportation or removal from DHS. A denial of the stay by DHS does not preclude an immigration judge or the BIA from granting a stay in connection with a previously filed motion to reopen or motion to reconsider. DHS shall take all reasonable steps to comply with a stay granted by an immigration judge or the BIA, but such a stay shall cease to have effect if granted or communicated after the noncitizen has been placed aboard an aircraft or other conveyance for removal and the normal boarding has been completed. 8 C.F.R. §§ 241.6, 1241.6.

In the context of bond proceedings, the BIA has the authority to grant a stay of the execution of an immigration judge's decision when DHS has appealed or provided notice of intent to appeal by filing the Notice of Service Intent to Appeal Custody Redetermination (Form EOIR-43) with the immigration court within one business day of the immigration judge's bond order, and files the appeal within 10 business days. The BIA may also entertain motions to reconsider discretionary stays it has granted. See 8 C.F.R. § 1003.19(i)(1)-(2); see also Chapter 9.3(f) (Appeals).

There are important differences between the automatic stay provisions in deportation and exclusion proceedings and the automatic stay provisions in removal proceedings. Other than a motion to reopen in absentia deportation proceedings, those differences are not covered in this Practice Manual. Accordingly, parties in deportation or exclusion proceedings should carefully review the controlling law and regulations.

8.2   Automatic Stays

There are certain circumstances when an immigration judge's order of removal is automatically stayed pending further action on an appeal or motion. When a stay is automatic, the immigration courts and the BIA do not issue a written order on the stay.

(a) During the Appeal Period — After an immigration judge issues a final decision on the merits of a case (not including bond or custody, credible fear, claimed status review, or reasonable fear determinations), the order is automatically stayed for the 30-day period for filing an appeal with the BIA. However, the order is not stayed if the losing party waived the right to appeal. 8 C.F.R. § 1003.6(a).

(b) During the Adjudication of an Appeal — If a party appeals an immigration judge's decision on the merits of the case (not including bond and custody determinations) to the BIA during the appeal period, the order of removal is automatically stayed during the BIA's adjudication of the appeal. 8 C.F.R. § 1003.6(a). The stay remains in effect until the BIA renders a final decision in the case.

(c) During the Adjudication of Case Certified to the BIA — A removal order is stayed while the BIA adjudicates a case that is before that appellate body by certification. 8 C.F.R. § 1003.6(a); see also Chapter 6.5 (Certification). The stay remains in effect until the BIA renders a final decision in the case or declines to accept certification of the case.

(d) Motions to Reopen —

(1) Removal proceedings — An immigration judge's removal order is stayed during the period between the filing of a motion to reopen removal proceedings conducted in absentia and the immigration judge's ruling on that motion. 8 C.F.R. § 1003.23(b)(4)(ii).

An immigration judge's removal order is automatically stayed during the BIA's adjudication of an appeal of the immigration judge's ruling in certain motions to reopen filed by battered spouses, children, and parents. INA § 240(c)(7)(C)(iv).

An immigration judge's order is not automatically stayed in appeals to the BIA from an immigration judge's denial of a motion to reopen removal proceedings conducted in absentia, and motions to reopen or reconsider a prior BIA decision are not automatically stayed.

(2) Deportation proceedings — An immigration judge's deportation order is stayed during the period between the filing of a motion to reopen deportation proceedings conducted in absentia under prior INA § 242B and the immigration judge's ruling on that motion, as well as during the adjudication by the BIA of any subsequent appeal of that motion. 8 C.F.R. § 1003.23(b)(4)(iii)(C).

Automatic stays only attach to the original appeal from an immigration judge's denial of a motion to reopen deportation proceedings conducted in absentia under prior INA § 242B. See 8 C.F.R. § 1003.23(b)(4)(iii)(C). Additionally, there is no automatic stay to a motion to reopen or reconsider the BIA's prior dismissal of an appeal from an immigration judge's denial of a motion to reopen deportation proceedings conducted in absentia under prior INA § 242B.

(e) Federal Court Remands — A federal court remand to the BIA results in an automatic stay of an order of removal if:

(1) The BIA's decision before the federal court involved a direct appeal of an immigration judge's decision on the merits of the case (excluding bond and custody determinations); or

(2) The BIA's decision before the federal court involved an appeal of an immigration judge's denial of a motion to reopen deportation proceedings conducted in absentia under prior INA § 242B.

8.3   Discretionary Stays

(a) Jurisdiction — Both immigration judges and the BIA have authority to grant and reconsider stays as a matter of discretion but only for matters within the judges' or the BIA's respective jurisdiction. See Chapters 1.4 (Jurisdiction and Authority), 9.3(b) (Jurisdiction). Immigration judges consider requests for discretionary stays only when a motion to reopen or a motion to reconsider is pending before the immigration court.

In most cases, the BIA entertains stays only when there is an appeal from an immigration judge's denial of a motion to reopen removal proceedings or a motion to reopen or reconsider a prior BIA decision pending before the BIA. The BIA may also consider a stay of an immigration judge's bond decision while a bond appeal is pending in order to prevent the noncitizen's release from detention. See Chapter 9.3(f) (Appeals).

(b) Motion to Reopen to Apply for Asylum, Withholding of Removal under the Act, or Protection under the Convention Against Torture — Time and numerical limitations do not apply to motions to reopen to apply for asylum, withholding of removal under the Act, or protection under the Convention Against Torture if the motion is based on changed country conditions arising in the country of nationality or the country to which removal has been ordered, if such evidence is material and was not available and could not have been discovered or presented at the previous proceeding. The filing of a motion to reopen in such circumstances does not automatically stay a noncitizen's removal. The noncitizen may request a stay and, if granted by the immigration court, shall not be removed pending disposition of the motion. If the original asylum application was denied based on a finding that it was frivolous, the noncitizen is ineligible to file a motion to reopen or reconsider or for a stay of removal. 8 C.F.R. § 1003.23(b)(4)(i).

When filing a motion to reopen to apply for asylum, withholding of removal under the Act, or protection under the Convention Against Torture based on changed country conditions, the noncitizen does not need to file a copy of their record of proceedings or A-file.

(c) Motion Required — Parties should submit a request for a discretionary stay by filing a written motion. The motion should comply with all the requirements for filing, including formatting, inclusion of a proof of service, and submission of possible fees. See Chapter 3 (Filing with the Immigration Court), Appendix E (Cover Pages).

(1) **Contents** — A party requesting a discretionary stay of removal before the immigration court should submit a motion stating the complete case history and all relevant facts. It should also include a copy of the order that the party wants stayed, if available. If the moving party does not have a copy of the order, that party should provide the date of the order and a detailed description of the immigration judge's ruling and reasoning, as articulated by the immigration judge. If the facts are in dispute, the moving party should provide appropriate evidence. See Chapter 5.2(e) (Evidence). A discretionary request to stay removal, deportation, or exclusion may be submitted at any time after a noncitizen

becomes subject to a final order of removal, deportation, or exclusion if a motion to reopen or reconsider is pending before the immigration court.

A party requesting a discretionary stay of removal, deportation, or exclusion before BIA should follow the procedures described below:

(A) Who may request — A respondent (or a respondent's practitioner of record) may request a discretionary stay of removal, deportation, or exclusion only if the respondent's case is currently before the BIA and the respondent is subject to a removal, deportation, or exclusion order.

(B) Timing of request — A request to stay removal, deportation, or exclusion may be submitted at any time during the pendency of a case before the BIA.

(C) Form of request — Requests to stay removal, deportation, or exclusion must be made in writing. The BIA prefers that stay requests be submitted in the form of a "MOTION TO STAY REMOVAL." See Appendix E (Cover Pages).

(D) Contents — The motion should contain a complete recitation of the relevant facts and case history and indicate the current status of the case. The motion must also contain a specific statement of the time exigencies involved. Motions containing vague or general statements of urgency are not persuasive.

A copy of the existing immigration judge or BIA order should be included, when available. When the moving party does not have a copy of the order, the moving party should provide the date of the immigration judge's decision and a detailed description of both the ruling and the basis of that ruling, as articulated by the immigration judge. If the facts are in dispute, the moving party should furnish evidence supporting the motion to stay.

(E) Format — The motion should comply with the general rules for filing motions. See Chapter 5.2 (Filing a Motion). The motion must include a Proof of Service. See Chapter 3.2 (Service on the Opposing Party), Appendix F (Cert. of Service).

(F) Fee — A motion to stay removal, deportation, or exclusion does not, by itself, require a filing fee. The underlying appeal or motion, however, may still require a fee. See Chapter 3.4 (Filing Fees).

(2) Emergency v. non-emergency — The immigration courts and the BIA categorize stay requests into two categories: emergency and non-emergency. When filing a stay request with the immigration court, the parties should submit their motion with a cover page either labeled "MOTION TO STAY REMOVAL" or "EMERGENCY MOTION TO STAY REMOVAL," as relevant.

(A) Emergency — The immigration courts and the BIA may rule immediately on an "emergency" stay request. The immigration court and the BIA only consider a stay request to be an emergency when a respondent is:

1. in DHS's physical custody and removal, deportation, or exclusion is imminent;

2. turning themselves in to DHS custody in order to be removed, deported, or excluded and removal, deportation, or exclusion is expected to occur within the next 3 business days; or

3. scheduled to self-execute an order of removal, deportation, or exclusion within the next 3 business days.

The motion should contain a specific statement of the time exigencies involved.

If a party is seeking an emergency stay from the BIA, the party must contact the BIA's Emergency Stay Unit by calling 703-306-0093. If a party is seeking an emergency stay from an immigration court, they must call the immigration court from which the removal order was issued. EOIR otherwise will not be able to properly process the request as an emergency stay. The BIA's Emergency Stay Unit is closed on federal holidays. It will consider an emergency stay request only on non-holiday weekdays from 9:00 a.m. to 5:30 p.m. (Eastern Time). Immigration courts will consider stay requests during posted operating hours.

A respondent may supplement a non-emergency stay request with an emergency stay request if qualifying circumstances, such as when a respondent reports to DHS custody for imminent removal, arise.

Parties can obtain instructions for filing an emergency stay motion with the BIA by calling the same numbers. For a list of immigration court numbers, see Appendix A (Directory) or visit EOIR's website.

When circumstances require immediate attention from the BIA or immigration courts, EOIR may, at the adjudicator's discretion, entertain a telephonic stay request.

EOIR promptly notifies the parties of its decision.

(B) Non-emergency — The immigration courts and the BIA do not rule immediately on a "non-emergency" stay request. Instead, the request is considered during the normal course of adjudication. Non-emergency stay requests include those from respondents who are not facing removal within the next 3 business days, and who are either:

1. not in detention; or

2. in detention but not facing imminent removal, deportation, or exclusion.

(d) Pending Motions — Neither the immigration judges nor the BIA automatically grant discretionary stays. The mere filing of a motion for a discretionary stay of an order does not prevent the execution of the order. Therefore, DHS may execute the underlying removal, deportation, or exclusion order unless and until the immigration judge or the BIA grants the motion for a stay.

(e) Adjudication and Notice — When an immigration judge or the BIA grants a discretionary stay of removal, deportation, or exclusion, the immigration judge or the BIA issues a written order. When a discretionary stay is granted, the parties are promptly notified about the decision.

(f) Duration — A discretionary stay of removal, deportation, or exclusion lasts until the immigration judge adjudicates the motion to reopen or motion to reconsider or until the BIA renders a final decision on the merits of the appeal, motion to reopen, or the motion to reconsider.

Chapter 9 Detention and Bond

9.1   Detention

(a) In General — The Department of Homeland Security (DHS) bears the responsibility for the apprehension and detention of noncitizens. Immigrations judges have jurisdiction over custody determinations under certain circumstances. See generally 8 C.F.R. § 1003.19. See also Chapter 9.3 (Bond Proceedings).

(b) Place and Conditions — Noncitizens may be detained in a Department of Homeland Security (DHS) Processing Facility, or in any public or private detention facility contracted by DHS to detain noncitizens. See 8 C.F.R. § 235.3(e). Immigration judges have no jurisdiction over the location of detention and the conditions in the detention facility.

(c) Appearance at Hearings — The Department of Homeland Security is responsible for ensuring that detained respondents appear at all hearings.

(d) Transfers and Release — The Department of Homeland Security (DHS) sometimes transfers detained respondents between detention facilities.

(1) Notification — DHS is obligated to notify the immigration court when a respondent is moved between detention locations. See 8 C.F.R. § 1003.19(g).

In addition, DHS is responsible for notifying the immigration court when a respondent is released from custody. See 8 C.F.R. § 1003.19(g). Nonetheless, the respondent should file a change of address form (Form EOIR-33/IC) with the immigration court to ensure that immigration court records are up to date.

(2) Venue — If a respondent has been transferred while proceedings are pending, the immigration judge with original jurisdiction over the case retains jurisdiction until that immigration judge grants a motion to change venue. Either DHS or the respondent may file a motion to change venue. See Chapter 5 (Motions before the Immigration Court). If DHS brings the respondent before an immigration judge in another immigration court and a motion to change venue has not been granted, the second immigration judge does not have jurisdiction over the case, except for bond redeterminations.

(e) Conduct of Hearing — Proceedings for detained respondents are expedited. Hearings are held either at the detention facility or at the immigration court, either by video or telephone conference. For more information on hearings conducted by video or telephone conference, see Chapter 4.7 (Hearings by Video or Telephone Conference).

(1) Special considerations for hearings in detention facilities — For hearings in detention facilities, parties must comply with the facility's security restrictions. See Chapter 4.14 (Access to Court).

(2) Orientation — In some detention facilities, detainees are provided with orientations or "rights presentations" by non-profit organizations. The Executive Office for Immigration Review also funds orientation programs at a number of

detention facilities, which are administered by the EOIR Legal Orientation Program. See Additional Reference Materials, Chapter 2.3 (Legal Orientation Program).

9.2   Detained Juveniles

(a) In General — There are special procedures for juveniles in federal custody, whether they are accompanied or unaccompanied. See generally 8 C.F.R. § 1236.3. For purposes of this chapter, a juvenile is defined as a noncitizen under 18 years of age. An unaccompanied juvenile is defined as a noncitizen under 18 years of age who does not have a parent or legal guardian in the United States to provide care and physical custody.

(b) Place and Conditions of Detention — The Department of Homeland Security (DHS) bears the initial responsibility for apprehension and detention of juveniles. When DHS determines that a juvenile is accompanied by a parent or legal guardian, DHS retains responsibility for the juvenile's detention and removal. When DHS determines that a juvenile is unaccompanied and must be detained, they are transferred to the care of the Department of Health and Human Services, Office of Refugee Resettlement, which provides for the care and placement, where possible, of the unaccompanied juvenile. See 6 U.S.C. § 279.

(c) Representation and Conduct of Hearing — For provisions regarding the representation of juveniles, and the conduct of hearings involving juveniles, see Chapter 4.22 (Juveniles).

(d) Release — Unaccompanied juveniles who are released from custody are released to a parent, a legal guardian, an adult relative who is not in Department of Homeland Security detention, or, in limited circumstances, to an adult who is not a family member.

9.3   Bond Proceedings

(a) In General — In certain circumstances, a noncitizen detained by the Department of Homeland Security (DHS) can be released from custody upon the payment of bond.

Initially, the bond is set by DHS. Upon the noncitizen's request, an immigration judge may conduct a "bond hearing," in which the immigration judge has the authority to redetermine the amount of bond set by DHS.

Bond proceedings are separate from removal proceedings. For guidance on entering an appearance in bond proceedings, see Chapter 2.1(b)(2) (Scope of Representation); see also generally 8 C.F.R. §§ 1003.17(a), 1003.19, 1236.1.

(b) Jurisdiction — Except as provided in subsections (1) through (3) below, an immigration judge generally has jurisdiction to conduct a bond hearing if the respondent is in Department of Homeland Security (DHS) custody. The immigration judge also has jurisdiction to conduct a bond hearing if the respondent is released from DHS custody upon payment of a bond and, within 7 days of release, files a request for a bond redetermination with the immigration court.

An immigration judge has jurisdiction over such cases even if a charging document has not been filed. In addition, an immigration judge has jurisdiction to rule on whether they have jurisdiction to conduct a bond hearing.

(1) No jurisdiction by regulation — By regulation, an immigration judge does not have jurisdiction to conduct bond hearings involving:

- noncitizens in exclusion proceedings

- "arriving aliens," as defined in 8 C.F.R. § 1001.1(q), in removal proceedings

- noncitizens ineligible for release on security or related grounds

- noncitizens ineligible for release on certain criminal grounds

8 C.F.R. § 1003.19(h)(2)(i).

(2) No jurisdiction by mootness — A bond becomes moot, and the immigration judge loses jurisdiction to conduct a bond hearing, when a noncitizen:

- departs from the United States, whether voluntarily or involuntarily

- is granted relief from removal by the immigration judge, and the Department of Homeland Security does not appeal

- is granted relief from removal by the Board of Immigration Appeals

- is denied relief from removal by the immigration judge, and the noncitizen does not appeal

- is denied relief from removal by the Board of Immigration Appeals

(3) Other — Immigration judges do not have bond jurisdiction in certain limited proceedings. See generally Chapter 7 (Other Proceedings before Immigration Judges).

(c) Requesting a Bond Hearing — A request for a bond hearing may be made in writing. In addition, except as provided in subsection (3), below, a request for a bond hearing may be made orally in court or, at the discretion of the immigration judge, by telephone. If available, a copy of the Notice to Appear (Form I-862) should be provided. The telephone number of each immigration court is listed on the EOIR website.

(1) Contents — A request for a bond hearing should state:

- the full name and A-number of the respondent

- the bond amount set by the Department of Homeland Security

- if the respondent is detained, the location of the detention facility

(2) No fee — There is no filing fee to request a bond hearing.

(3) Where to request — A request for a bond hearing is made, in order of preference, to:

- if the respondent is detained, the immigration court having jurisdiction over the respondent's place of detention;

- the immigration court with administrative control over the case; or

- the Office of the Chief Immigration Judge for designation of an appropriate immigration court

8 C.F.R. § 1003.19(c). See Chapter 3.1(a)(1) (Administrative control courts).

(4) Multiple requests — If an immigration judge or the Board of Immigration Appeals has previously ruled in bond proceedings involving a respondent, a subsequent request for a bond hearing must be in writing, and the respondent must show that their circumstances have changed materially since the last decision. In addition, the request must comply with the requirements listed in subsection (c)(1), above. 8 C.F.R. § 1003.19(e).

(d) Scheduling a Hearing — In general, after receiving a request for a bond hearing, the immigration court schedules the hearing for the earliest possible date and notifies the respondent and the Department of Homeland Security.

In limited circumstances, an immigration judge may rule on a bond redetermination request without holding a hearing.

If a respondent requests a bond hearing during another type of hearing (for example, during a master calendar hearing in removal proceedings), the immigration judge may:

- stop the other hearing and conduct a bond hearing on that date

- complete the other hearing and conduct a bond hearing on that date

- complete the other hearing and schedule a bond hearing for a later date

- stop the other hearing and schedule a bond hearing for a later date

(e) Bond Hearings — In a bond hearing, the immigration judge determines whether the respondent is eligible for bond. If the respondent is eligible for bond, the immigration judge considers whether respondent's release would pose a danger to property or persons, whether the respondent is likely to appear for further immigration proceedings, and whether the respondent is a threat to national security. In general, bond hearings are less formal than hearings in removal proceedings.

(1) Location — Generally, a bond hearing is held at the immigration court where the request for bond redetermination is filed.

(2) Representation — In a bond hearing, the respondent may be represented by a practitioner of record at no expense to the government.

(3) Generally not recorded — Bond hearings are generally not recorded.

(4) Record of Proceedings — The immigration judge creates a record, which is kept separate from the Records of Proceedings for other immigration court proceedings involving the respondent.

(5) Evidence — Documents for the immigration judge to consider are filed in open court or, if the request for a bond hearing was made in writing, together with the request. Since the Record of Proceedings in a bond proceeding is kept separate and apart from other Records of Proceedings, documents already filed in removal proceedings must be resubmitted if the filing party wishes them to be considered in the bond proceeding.

If documents are filed in advance of the hearing, the documents should be filed *together with* the request for a bond hearing. If a document is filed in advance of the hearing but separate from the request for a bond hearing, it should be filed with a cover page labeled "BOND PROCEEDINGS." See Appendix E (Cover Pages).

Unless otherwise directed by the immigration judge, the deadlines and requirements for filings in Chapter 3 (Filing with the Immigration Court) do not apply in bond proceedings.

(6) Conduct of hearing — While the immigration judge decides how each hearing is conducted, parties should submit relevant evidence and:

- the Department of Homeland Security (DHS) should state whether a bond has been set and, if a bond has been set, the amount of the bond and the DHS justification for that amount

- the respondent or the respondent's practitioner of record should make an oral statement (an "offer of proof" or "proffer") addressing whether the respondent's release would pose a danger to property or persons, whether the respondent is likely to appear for future immigration proceedings, and whether the respondent poses a danger to national security

At the immigration judge's discretion, witnesses may be placed under oath and testimony taken. However, parties should be mindful that bond hearings are generally briefer and less formal than hearings in removal proceedings.

(7) Decision — The immigration judge's decision is based on any information that is available to the immigration judge or that is presented by the parties. See 8 C.F.R. § 1003.19(d).

Usually, the immigration judge's decision is rendered orally. Because bond hearings are generally not recorded, the decision is not transcribed. If either party appeals, the immigration judge prepares a written decision based on notes from the hearing.

(f) Appeals — Either party may appeal the immigration judge's decision to the Board of Immigration Appeals. If the respondent appeals, the immigration judge's bond decision remains in effect while the appeal is pending. If the Department of Homeland Security appeals, the immigration judge's bond decision remains in effect while the appeal is pending unless the Board issues an emergency stay or the decision is automatically stayed by regulation. See 8 C.F.R. §§ 1003.6(c), 1003.19(i).

For detailed guidance on when immigration judges' decisions in bond proceedings are stayed, parties should consult the Board of Immigration Appeals Practice Manual, which is available on the Executive Office for Immigration Review website at the EOIR website.

9.4   Detention Review

(a) In General — Generally, the Department of Homeland Security (DHS) must remove or release detained respondents within 90 days of a final order of removal. However, DHS may continue to detain a respondent whose removal from the United States is not "reasonably foreseeable," if the respondent's release would pose a special danger to the public. See INA § 241(a)(6), 8 C.F.R. § 1241.14(f). Such a decision by DHS to continue to detain a respondent is reviewed by an immigration judge in "continued detention review proceedings." While background investigations and security checks are not required, as custody decisions require promptness, the regulations do allow for some consideration of these matters: "[i]n scheduling an initial custody redetermination hearing, the immigration judge shall, to the extent practicable consistent with the expedited nature of such cases, take account of the brief initial period of time needed for DHS to conduct the automated portions of its identity, law enforcement, or security investigations or examinations with respect to [noncitizens] detained in connection with immigration proceedings." 8 C.F.R § 1003.47(k). The proceedings begin with a DHS determination that continued detention is required and are divided into two phases: (1) reasonable cause hearings and (2) continued detention review merits hearings. See subsections (c), (d), below.

(b) DHS Determination — If a respondent has been ordered removed but remains detained, they may request that the Department of Homeland Security (DHS) determine whether there is a significant likelihood of removal in the reasonably foreseeable future. See 8 C.F.R. § 241.13. If there is a significant likelihood of removal in the reasonably foreseeable future, DHS may continue to detain the respondent.

If there is *not* a significant likelihood of removal in the reasonably foreseeable future, the respondent is released unless DHS determines, based on a full medical and physical examination, including a mental-health evaluation, that the respondent should be subject to continued detention because the respondent's release would pose a special danger to the public. Following such a determination, the matter is referred to an immigration judge for a reasonable cause hearing. See 8 C.F.R. § 1241.14(f).

(c) Reasonable Cause Hearing — A reasonable cause hearing is a brief hearing to evaluate the evidence supporting the determination by the Department of Homeland Security (DHS) that the respondent's release would pose a special danger to the public. In the hearing, the immigration judge decides whether DHS's evidence is sufficient to establish reasonable cause to go forward with a continued detention review merits hearing, or whether the respondent should be released. See generally 8 C.F.R. § 1241.14.

(1) Initiation — Jurisdiction vests with the immigration court when DHS files a Form I-863 (Notice of Referral to the immigration judge) with the court having jurisdiction over the place of the respondent's custody.

(2) Timing — The reasonable cause hearing begins no later than 10 business days after referral to the immigration court. These hearings must take priority over all other hearings with the exception of credible fear review hearings.

(3) Location — If possible, the reasonable cause hearing is conducted in person, but may be conducted by telephone conference or video conference, at the immigration judge's discretion. See Chapter 4.7 (Hearings by Video or Telephone Conference).

(4) Representation — The respondent is provided with a list of free or low-cost legal service providers and may be represented by a practitioner of record at no expense to the government.

(5) Conduct of hearing — At the outset of the hearing, the immigration judge will explain the respondent's rights to the respondent, including a reasonable opportunity to examine evidence and witnesses presented by DHS, and to present evidence on their own behalf. DHS may offer any evidence that is material and relevant to the proceeding. EOIR will provide an interpreter for the hearing.

(6) Record of Proceedings — The immigration judge creates a Record of Proceedings, and the hearing is recorded. The Record of Proceedings is not combined with records of any other immigration court proceedings involving the same respondent.

(7) Immigration judge's decision — If the immigration judge finds that DHS has met its burden of showing reasonable cause to go forward with a continued detention review merits hearing, the respondent is notified, and the merits hearing is scheduled.

If the immigration judge finds that DHS has *not* met its burden, the immigration judge dismisses the proceedings, and the respondent is released under conditions determined by DHS.

The immigration judge will render a decision in oral or written form. An oral decision will be made on the record, in summary form. The oral decision must be identified as "the decision of the immigration judge."

Written (reserved) decisions must be issued within five business days after the close of the record, unless that time period is extended 1) by an agreement of both parties; 2) because of a delay caused by the respondent; or 3) by a determination by the Chief Immigration Judge that "exceptional circumstances make it impractical to render the decision on a highly expedited basis." Approval for an extension based upon certification by the Chief Immigration Judge must be obtained no later than the third business day after the hearing is concluded.

(8) Appeals — If the immigration judge finds that DHS has not met its burden of showing reasonable cause to go forward with a continued detention review merits hearing, DHS may appeal to the Board of Immigration Appeals. The appeal must be filed within two business days after the immigration judge's order. The immigration judge's order dismissing the proceedings is stayed pending adjudication of an appeal, unless DHS waives the right to appeal. If the Board of Immigration Appeals determines that DHS has met its burden, the case will be remanded to the immigration judge to conduct a continued review detention merits hearing, scheduled to commence within 30 days from the Board's order.

If the immigration judge finds that DHS *has* met its burden, the decision is not appealable by the respondent.

(d) Continued Detention Review Merits Hearing — In the continued detention review merits hearing, the Department of Homeland Security (DHS) has the burden of proving by clear and convincing evidence that the respondent should remain in custody because the respondent's release would pose a special danger to the public. See generally 8 C.F.R. § 1241.14.

(1) Initiation — The immigration court's jurisdiction vests for a continued detention review merits hearing after either the immigration court or the Board, pursuant to a final decision in a reasonable cause hearing, has determined that DHS's determination and evidence is sufficient to establish reasonable cause to proceed with a continued detention review merits hearing.

(2) Timing — The continued detention review merits hearing is scheduled promptly. If the respondent requests, the merits hearing is scheduled to commence within 30 days of the decision in the reasonable cause hearing.

(3) Representation — The respondent is provided with a list of free and low-cost legal service providers and may be represented by a practitioner of record at no expense to the government.

(4) Conduct of hearing — The immigration judge may receive into evidence any oral or written statement that is material and relevant to the proceeding. The ROP that was used for the reasonable cause hearing will also be used for the continued detention review merits hearing. The respondent has the right to be represented at no cost to the government by a practitioner of record and shall be given a list of free legal service providers. The respondent has a reasonable opportunity to examine evidence against them, to present evidence and witnesses on their own behalf, and to cross-examine witnesses presented by DHS. In addition, the respondent has the right to cross-examine the author of any medical or mental health reports used as a basis for DHS's determination that the respondent's release would pose a special danger to the public. In addition to receiving a written statement of rights, the immigration judge will explain these rights to the respondent at the beginning of the hearing.

(5) Immigration judge's decision — If the immigration judge determines that DHS has met its burden of showing that the respondent should remain in custody as a special danger to the public, the immigration judge orders the continued detention of the respondent.

If the immigration judge determines that DHS has *not* met its burden, the immigration judge dismisses the proceedings, and the respondent is released under conditions determined by DHS.

The immigration judge may render either an oral or written (reserved) decision. Written decisions must be issued within ten days after the close of the record, subject to extension pursuant to the same procedures as those for reasonable cause hearings.

(6) Appeals — Either party may appeal the immigration judge's decision to the Board of Immigration Appeals. Appeals by DHS must be filed within 5 business days of the immigration judge's order. Appeals by respondents are subject to the same deadlines as appeals in removal proceedings. For detailed guidance on appeals, parties should consult the Board of Immigration Appeals Practice Manual, Chapter 4 (Appeals of Immigration Judge Decisions), which is available on the Executive Office for Immigration Review website at the EOIR website.

If the immigration judge dismisses the proceedings and orders the respondent released, the order is stayed pending adjudication of any DHS appeal, unless DHS waives the right to appeal.

(e) Periodic Review — Following proceedings in which the respondent's continued detention has been ordered, the respondent may periodically request that the Department of Homeland Security (DHS) review their continued detention. The respondent must show that, due to a material change in circumstances, the respondent's release would no longer pose a special danger to the public. Such requests may be made no earlier than 6 months after the most recent decision of the immigration judge or the Board of Immigration Appeals.

If DHS does not release the respondent, the respondent may file a motion with the immigration court to set aside its prior determination in the proceedings. The respondent must show that, due to a material change in circumstances, the respondent's release would no longer pose a special danger to the public. If the immigration judge grants the motion, a new continued detention review merits hearing will be scheduled to be held within 30 days of the grant of the motion. If the motion is denied, the respondent may appeal to the Board.

This page intentionally left blank.

Chapter 10 Discipline of Practitioners

10.1 Practitioner Discipline Generally

The Executive Office for Immigration Review has the authority to impose disciplinary sanctions on practitioners and recognized organizations who violate rules of professional conduct in practice before the immigration courts, the Board of Immigration Appeals, and the Department of Homeland Security. See 8 C.F.R. §§ 292.3, 1003.1(d)(2)(iii), 1003.1(d)(5), 1003.101-111. See also *Matter of Gadda*, 23 I&N Dec. 645 (BIA 2003)

Generally, discipline of practitioners and recognized organizations is initiated by the filing of a complaint. See Chapter 10.5 (Filing a Complaint). Any individual, including immigration judges, may file a complaint about the conduct of a practitioner or recognized organization.

10.2 Definition of Practitioner and Recognized Organization

The term "practitioner" refers to a noncitizen's attorney or representative, as defined in 8 C.F.R. §§ 1001.1(f), 1001.1(j), and 1292.1(a)-(b), respectively. The term "representative" refers to non-attorneys authorized to practice before the immigration courts and the Board of Immigration Appeals, including law students and law graduates, reputable individuals, accredited representatives, accredited officials, and persons formerly authorized to practice. See 8 C.F.R. §§ 1001.1(j), 1292.1(a)-(b). See also Chapter 2 (Appearances before the Immigration Court).

The term "recognized organization" is defined as a non-profit, federal tax-exempt, religious, charitable, social service, or similar organization established in the United States that has been recognized by the Assistant Director for Policy or the Assistant Director's designee to represent noncitizens through accredited representatives before DHS only or before the Board, the immigration courts, and DHS. See 8 C.F.R. § 1292.11.

10.3 Jurisdiction

(a) Immigration Judges — Immigration judges have the authority to file complaints concerning practitioners who appear before them.

The disciplinary procedures described in this chapter do not apply to immigration judges. For information on immigration judge conduct, see Chapter 1.3(c) (Immigration Judge Conduct and Professionalism).

(b) Practitioners — The disciplinary procedures described in this chapter apply to practitioners who practice before the immigration courts, the Board of Immigration Appeals, or the Department of Homeland Security. See 8 C.F.R. § 1003.101.

(c) Recognized Organizations — EOIR is authorized to discipline a recognized organization if it finds it to be in the public interest to do so. 8 C.F.R. § 1003.110. It is in the public interest to discipline a recognized organization that violates one or more of the grounds specified in 8 C.F.R. § 1003.110(b). Specific grounds for discipline of recognized organizations are listed in Chapter 10.4(b) (Recognized Organizations).

(d) DHS Attorneys — The disciplinary procedures described in this chapter do not apply to attorneys who represent the Department of Homeland Security (DHS). The conduct of DHS attorneys is governed by DHS rules and regulations. Concerns or complaints about the conduct of DHS attorneys may be raised in writing with the DHS Office of the Chief Counsel where the immigration court is located. A list of Offices of the Chief Counsel is available on the DHS, U.S. Immigration and Customs Enforcement website at www.ice.gov.

(e) Unauthorized Practice of Law — The disciplinary procedures described in this chapter apply to *practitioners* who assist in the unauthorized practice of law. See 8 C.F.R. § 1003.102(m). Anyone may file a complaint against a practitioner who is assisting in the unauthorized practice of law. See Chapter 10.5 (Filing a Complaint).

The disciplinary procedures described in this chapter do not apply to *non-practitioners* engaged in the unauthorized practice of law. Anyone harmed by an individual practicing law without authorization should contact the appropriate law enforcement or consumer protection agency. In addition, persons harmed by such conduct are encouraged to contact the Executive Office for Immigration Review Fraud and Abuse Prevention Program. See Additional Reference Materials, Chapter 8 (EOIR Fraud and Abuse Prevention Program), Appendix A (Directory).

In general, the unauthorized practice of law includes certain instances where non-attorneys perform legal services, give legal advice, or represent themselves to be attorneys. Individuals engaged in the unauthorized practice of law include some immigration specialists/consultants, visa consultants, and "notarios."

10.4 Conduct

(a) Practitioners — Conduct by practitioners that may result in discipline includes the following:

- grossly excessive fees;
- bribery or coercion;
- offering false evidence, or making a false statement of material fact or law;
- improperly soliciting clients;
- disbarment or suspension, or resignation while a disciplinary investigation or proceeding is pending;
- misrepresenting qualifications or services offered;
- action that would constitute contempt of court in a judicial proceeding;
- conviction for a serious crime;
- falsely certifying a copy of a document;
- frivolous behavior, as defined in 8 C.F.R. § 1003.102(j);
- ineffective assistance of counsel;

- repeated failure to appear;

- assisting in the unauthorized practice of law;

- engaging in conduct that is prejudicial to the administration of justice or undermines the integrity of the adjudicative process;

- failing to provide competent representation to a client;

- failing to abide by a client's decisions;

- failing to act with reasonable diligence and promptness;

- failing to control and manage the workload so that each matter can be handled competently;

- failing to comply with all time and filing limitations;

- failing to carry through to conclusion all matters undertaken for a client, consistent with the scope of representation;

- failing to maintain communication with the client;

- failing to disclose adverse legal authority;

- repeatedly failing to submit a signed and completed appearance form in compliance with the applicable rules and regulations; or

- repeatedly drafting boilerplate submissions that are filed with EOIR; or

- repeatedly failing to sign any pleading, application, motion, petition, brief, or other document that the practitioner prepared or drafted and was filed with EOIR.

For a full explanation of each ground for discipline, consult the regulations at 8 C.F.R. § 1003.102.

(b) Recognized Organizations — Conduct by recognized organizations which may result in discipline includes the following:

- knowingly or with reckless disregard providing a false statement or misleading information in applying for recognition or accreditation of its representative;

- knowingly or with reckless disregard providing false statements or misleading information to clients or prospective clients regarding the scope of its authority or services;

- failing to provide adequate supervision of accredited representatives;

- employing, or receiving services from, or affiliating with, an individual who performs an activity that constitutes the unauthorized practice of law or immigration fraud; or

- engaging in the practice of law through staff when the organization does not have an attorney or accredited representative.

For a full explanation of each ground for discipline, consult the regulations at 8 C.F.R. § 1003.110(b).

10.5 Filing a Complaint

(a) **Who May File** — Anyone may file a complaint against a practitioner or recognized organization, including immigration judges, Board Members, the practitioner's clients, Department of Homeland Security personnel, and other practitioners. 8 C.F.R. §§ 1003.104(a)(1), 1292.19(a).

(b) **What to File** — Complaints must be submitted in writing. Persons filing complaints are encouraged to use the Immigration Practitioner Complaint Form, (Form EOIR-44). See Chapter 11.2 (Obtaining Blank Forms); Appendix D (Forms). The Form EOIR-44 provides important information about the complaint process, the confidentiality of complaints, and the types of misconduct that can result in discipline by the Executive Office for Immigration Review. Complaints should be specific and as detailed as possible, and supporting documentation should be provided if available.

(c) **Where to File** — Complaints alleging practitioner misconduct before the immigration courts or the Board of Immigration Appeals, or complaints against recognized organizations, should be filed with the Executive Office for Immigration Review disciplinary counsel. 8 C.F.R. §§ 1003.104(a)(1), 1292.19(a). The completed Form EOIR-44 and supporting documents should be sent to:

United States Department of Justice
Executive Office for Immigration Review
Office of the General Counsel
5107 Leesburg Pike, Suite 2600
Falls Church, VA 22041
Attn: Disciplinary Counsel

OR

EOIR.Attorney.Discipline@usdoj.gov

See Appendix A (Directory). After receiving a complaint, the EOIR disciplinary counsel decides whether to initiate disciplinary proceedings. 8 C.F.R. §§ 1003.104(b), 1292.19(b). See Chapter 10.7 (Disciplinary Proceedings).

(d) **When to File** — Complaints should be filed as soon as possible. There are no time limits for filing most complaints. However, complaints based on ineffective assistance of counsel must be filed within one year of a finding of ineffective assistance of counsel by an immigration judge, the Board of Immigration Appeals, or a federal court judge or panel. 8 C.F.R. § 1003.102(k).

10.6 Duty to Report

A practitioner who practices before the immigration courts, the Board of Immigration Appeals, the Department of Homeland Security, and, if applicable, the authorized officer of each recognized organization with which a practitioner is affiliated, has an affirmative duty to report whenever the practitioner:

- has been found guilty of, or pled guilty or *nolo contendere* to, a serious crime (as defined in 8 C.F.R. § 1003.102(h)); or

- has been disbarred or suspended from practicing law or has resigned while a disciplinary investigation or proceeding is pending.

8 C.F.R. §§ 1003.103(c), 292.3(c)(4). The practitioner and, if applicable, the authorized officer of each recognized organization, must report the misconduct, criminal conviction, or discipline to the Executive Office for Immigration Review disciplinary counsel within 30 days of the issuance of the relevant initial order. This duty applies even if an appeal of the conviction or discipline is pending. Disciplinary counsel may be reached at the mailing and email address listed above.

10.7   Disciplinary Proceedings

(a) In General — Disciplinary proceedings take place in certain instances where a complaint against a practitioner or recognized organization is filed with the Executive Office for Immigration Review disciplinary counsel, or a practitioner or recognized organization self-reports. See Chapters 10.5 (Filing a Complaint), 10.6 (Duty to Report). See generally 8 C.F.R. §§ 1003.101-109.

In some cases, practitioners are subject to summary disciplinary proceedings, which involve distinct procedures as described in subsection (g), below.

In general, disciplinary hearings are conducted in the same manner as immigration court proceedings, as appropriate. 8 C.F.R. § 1003.106(a)(2)(v).

(b) Preliminary Investigation — When a complaint against a practitioner or recognized organization is filed, or a practitioner or recognized organization self-reports, the Executive Office for Immigration Review disciplinary counsel conducts a preliminary investigation. Upon concluding the investigation, the EOIR disciplinary counsel may elect to:

- take no further action;

- issue a warning letter or informal admonition to the practitioner;

- enter into an agreement in lieu of discipline; or

- initiate disciplinary proceedings by filing a Notice of Intent to Discipline (NID) with the Board of Immigration Appeals and serving a copy on the practitioner or recognized organization.

(c) Notice of Intent to Discipline — Except as described in subsection (g), below, the Notice of Intent to Discipline (NID) contains the charge(s), the preliminary inquiry report, proposed disciplinary sanctions, instructions for filing an answer and requesting a hearing, and the mailing address and telephone number of the Board of Immigration Appeals.

(1) Petition for Immediate Suspension — In certain circumstances, the Executive Office for Immigration Review disciplinary counsel files a petition with the Board of Immigration Appeals to immediately suspend the practitioner from practicing before the immigration courts and the Board. These circumstances include a conviction of a serious crime, disbarment or suspension from practicing law, or resignation while disciplinary proceedings are pending. Practitioners subject to a petition for immediate suspension are placed in summary disciplinary proceedings, as described in subsection (g), below.

The Board may set aside such a suspension upon good cause shown, if doing so is in the interest of justice. The hardships that typically accompany suspension from practice, such as loss of income and inability to complete pending cases, are usually insufficient to set aside a suspension order.

(2) DHS motion to join in disciplinary proceedings — The Department of Homeland Security (DHS) may file a motion to join in the disciplinary proceedings. If the motion is granted, any suspension or disbarment from practice before the immigration courts and the Board of Immigration Appeals will also apply to practice before DHS.

(3) Petition for Interim Suspension — In certain circumstances, the Executive Office for Immigration Review Disciplinary Counsel may petition for an interim suspension from practice of an accredited representative before the Board and the immigration courts. 8 C.F.R. § 1003.111(a)(1). DHS may ask that the accredited representative be similarly suspended from practice before DHS. 8 C.F.R. § 1003.111(a)(2).

The petition must demonstrate by a preponderance of the evidence that the accredited representative poses a substantial threat of irreparable harm to clients or prospective clients. See 8 C.F.R. § 1003.111(a)(3).

(d) Answer — A practitioner or recognized organization subject to a Notice of Intent to Discipline (NID) has 30 days from the date of service to file a written answer with the Board of Immigration Appeals and serve a copy on the counsel for the government. See Chapter 3.2 (Service on the Opposing Party). The answer is deemed filed when it is *received* by the Board.

(1) Contents — In the answer, the practitioner, or, in cases involving recognized organizations, the organization, must admit or deny each allegation in the NID. Each allegation not expressly denied is deemed admitted. In addition, the answer must state whether the practitioner or recognized organization requests a hearing. If a hearing is not requested, the opportunity to request a hearing is deemed waived. 8 C.F.R. § 1003.105(c)(2).

(2) Motion for extension of time to answer — The deadline for filing an answer may be extended for good cause shown, pursuant to a written motion filed with the Board of Immigration Appeals no later than 3 working days before the deadline. The motion should be filed with a cover page labeled "MOTION FOR EXTENSION OF TIME TO ANSWER" and comply with the requirements for filing. For information on the requirements for filing with the Board, parties should consult the Board of Immigration Appeals Practice Manual, which is available at the EOIR website.

(3) Default order — If the practitioner or, in cases involving recognized organizations, the organization, does not file a timely answer, the Board of Immigration Appeals issues a default order imposing the discipline proposed in the NID, unless special considerations are present. 8 C.F.R. § 1003.105(d)(2).

(4) Motion to set aside default order — A practitioner or, in cases involving recognized organizations, the organization, subject to a default order may file a written motion with the Board of Immigration Appeals to set aside a default order. The motion to set aside a default order must be filed within 15 days of service of the default order. 8 C.F.R. § 1003.105(d)(2). The motion should be filed with a cover page labeled "MOTION TO SET ASIDE DEFAULT ORDER" and comply with the requirements for filing. For information on the requirements for filing with the Board, parties should consult the Board of Immigration Appeals Practice Manual.

The motion must show that the failure to file a timely answer was caused by exceptional circumstances beyond the control the practitioner or recognized organization, such as the serious illness or the death of an immediate relative, but not including less compelling circumstances. 8 C.F.R. § 1003.105(d)(2).

(e) Adjudication — Except as described in subsection (g) below, if a practitioner, or, in cases involving recognized organizations, the organization, files a timely answer, the matter is referred to an immigration judge or Administrative Law Judge who will act as the adjudicating official in the disciplinary proceedings. An immigration judge cannot adjudicate a matter in which they filed the complaint or which involves a practitioner who regularly appears in front of that immigration judge.

(1) Adjudication without hearing — If the practitioner or recognized organization files a timely answer without a request for a hearing, the adjudicating official provides the parties with the opportunity to file briefs and evidence to support or refute any of the charges or affirmative defenses, and the matter is adjudicated without a hearing.

(2) Adjudication with hearing — If the practitioner or recognized organization files a timely answer with a request for a hearing, a hearing is conducted as described in subsections (A) through (E), below.

(A) Timing and location — The time and place of the hearing is designated with due regard to all relevant factors, including the location of the practitioner's practice or residence or, in the case of a recognized organization, the location of the recognized organization, and the convenience of witnesses. The practitioner or the recognized organization is afforded adequate time to prepare the case in advance of the hearing.

(B) Representation — The practitioner or, in cases involving recognized organizations, the organization, may be represented by a practitioner at no expense to the government.

(C) Pre-hearing conferences — Pre-hearing conferences may be held to narrow issues, obtain stipulations between the parties, exchange information voluntarily, or otherwise simplify and organize the proceeding.

(D) Timing of submissions — Deadlines for filings in disciplinary proceedings are as follows, unless otherwise specified by the adjudicating official. Filings must be submitted at least thirty (30) days in advance of the hearing. Responses to filings that were submitted in advance of a hearing must be filed within fifteen (15) days after the original filing.

(E) Conduct of hearing — At the hearing, each party has a reasonable opportunity to present evidence and witnesses, to examine and object to the other party's evidence, and to cross-examine the other party's witnesses.

(3) Decision — In rendering a decision, the adjudicating official considers the complaint, the preliminary inquiry report, the Notice of Intent to Discipline, the practitioner's, or, in cases involving recognized organizations, the organization's, answer, pleadings, briefs, evidence, any supporting documents, and any other materials.

(4) Sanctions authorized — A broad range of sanctions are authorized, including disbarment from immigration practice, suspension from immigration practice, and public or private censure. 8 C.F.R. § 1003.101(a).

The Executive Office for Immigration Review is also authorized to impose sanctions against a recognized organization, including revocation, termination, and such other sanctions as deemed appropriate. 8 C.F.R. § 1003.110.

(5) Appeal — The decision of the adjudicating official may be appealed to the Board of Immigration Appeals. A party wishing to appeal must file a Notice of Appeal from a Decision of an Adjudicating Official in a Practitioner Disciplinary Case (Form EOIR-45). See Chapter 11.2 (Obtaining Blank Forms), Appendix D (Forms). The Form EOIR-45 is specific to disciplinary proceedings. The Form EOIR-45 must be received by the Board no later than 30 calendar days after the adjudicating official renders an oral decision or mails a written decision. The parties must comply with all of the other standard provisions (non ECAS-related) for filing appeals with the Board. 8 C.F.R. § 1003.106(c). See Board of Immigration Appeals Practice Manual, Chapter 4 (Appeals of Immigration Judge Decisions).

Parties should note that, on appeal, the Board may increase the sanction imposed by the adjudicating official. See *Matter of Gadda*, 23 I&N Dec. 645 (BIA 2003).

(f) Where to File Documents — Documents in disciplinary proceedings should be filed as described below.

(1) Board of Immigration Appeals — When disciplinary proceedings are pending before the Board of Immigration Appeals, documents should be filed with the Board. For the Board's mailing address, parties should consult the Board of Immigration Appeals Practice Manual, which is available on the EOIR website. Examples of when to file documents with the Board include:

- after the filing of a Notice of Intent to Discipline, but before an adjudicating official is appointed to the case

- after a default order has been entered

- after an appeal has been filed

(2) Adjudication — When disciplinary proceedings are pending before an adjudicating official, documents should be sent to:

United States Department of Justice
Executive Office for Immigration Review
Office of the Chief Immigration Judge
5107 Leesburg Pike, Suite 2400
Falls Church, VA 22041
Attn: Chief Clerk of the Immigration Court

(g) Summary Disciplinary Proceedings — Summary disciplinary proceedings are held in cases where a petition for immediate suspension has been filed. See (c)(1), above. A preliminary inquiry report is not required to be filed with the Notice of Intent to Discipline (NID) in summary disciplinary proceedings.

These proceedings are conducted as described above, except that for the case to be referred to an adjudicating official, the practitioner must demonstrate in the answer to the NID that there is a material issue of fact in dispute or that certain special considerations are present. If the practitioner's answer meets this requirement, disciplinary proceedings are held as described in subsections (d) through (f), above. If the practitioner fails to meet this requirement, the Board issues an order imposing discipline. For additional information, see 8 C.F.R. §§ 1003.103(b), 1003.106(a).

10.8   Notice to Public

(a) Disclosure Generally Authorized — In general, action taken on a Notice of Intent to Discipline may be disclosed to the public. See 8 C.F.R. § 1003.108(c).

(b) Lists of Disciplined Practitioners — Lists of practitioners who have been disbarred, suspended, or publicly censured are posted at the immigration courts, at the Board of Immigration Appeals, and on the EOIR website. These lists are updated periodically.

10.9   Effect on Practitioner's Pending Immigration Cases

(a) Duty to Advise Clients — A practitioner or recognized organization that is disciplined is obligated to advise all clients whose cases are pending before the immigration courts, the Board of Immigration Appeals, or the Department of Homeland Security that the practitioner or recognized organization has been disciplined.

(b) Pending Cases Deemed Unrepresented — Once a practitioner has been disbarred or suspended, the practitioner's pending cases are deemed unrepresented. The immigration court rejects filings that are submitted by a practitioner after they have been disbarred or suspended. See Chapter 3.1(d) (Defective Filings).

(c) Ineffective Assistance of Counsel — The imposition of discipline on a practitioner does not, by itself, constitute evidence of ineffective assistance of counsel in the practitioner's former cases.

(d) Filing Deadlines — An order of practitioner or recognized organization discipline does not automatically excuse parties from meeting any applicable filing deadlines.

10.10 Reinstatement

(a) Following Suspension — Following a suspension, reinstatement is not automatic. With exceptions for accredited representatives specified in subsection (d) below, to be reinstated following a suspension, a practitioner must:

- file a motion with the Board of Immigration Appeals requesting to be reinstated;

- show that they are an attorney or representative as defined in 8 C.F.R. §§ 1001.1(f) and 1001.1(j), respectively; and

- serve a copy of the motion on the EOIR Disciplinary Counsel and the DHS Disciplinary Counsel.

8 C.F.R. § 1003.107(a)(1).

The Executive Office for Immigration Review Disciplinary Counsel or the DHS Disciplinary Counsel may file a written response, including supporting documents or evidence, objecting to reinstatement on the ground that the practitioner failed to comply with the terms of the suspension. 8 C.F.R. § 1003.107(a)(2). Failure to meet the definition of an attorney or accredited representative will result in the request for reinstatement being denied. 8 C.F.R. § 1003.107(b)(3). If the practitioner failed to comply with the terms of the suspension, the Board will deny the motion and indicate the circumstances under which reinstatement may be sought.

(b) During Suspension for More than One Year — A practitioner suspended for more than one year may file a petition for reinstatement with the Board of Immigration Appeals after one year has passed or one-half of the suspension has elapsed, whichever is greater. The practitioner must serve a copy of the petition on the Executive Office for Immigration Review disciplinary counsel. In the petition, the practitioner must show that:

- they are an attorney or representative as defined in 8 C.F.R. §§ 1001.1(f) and 1001.1(g), respectively;

- they possess the moral and professional qualifications required to appear before the Board, the immigration courts, or DHS; and

- their reinstatement will not be detrimental to the administration of justice.

8 C.F.R. § 1003.107(b).

The Board has the discretion to hold a hearing to determine if the practitioner meets all of the requirements for reinstatement. If the Board denies a petition for reinstatement, the practitioner is barred from filing a subsequent petition for reinstatement for one year from the date of denial.

(c) If Disbarred — A practitioner who has been disbarred may file a petition for reinstatement with the Board of Immigration Appeals after one year has passed, under the provisions described in subsection (b), above.

(d) Accredited Representatives —

(1) Suspended — When an accredited representative is suspended past the expiration of the period of accreditation, the representative may not seek reinstatement. After the representative's suspension period has expired, a new request for accreditation may be submitted by the recognized organization pursuant to 8 C.F.R. §§ 1003.107(c)(1), 1292.13.

(2) Disbarred — An accredited representative who has been disbarred may not seek reinstatement. 8 C.F.R. § 1003.107(c)(2).

(e) Cases Pending at Reinstatement — Suspension or disbarment terminates representation. A practitioner reinstated to immigration practice who wishes to represent clients as the practitioner of record before the immigration court, the Board of Immigration Appeals, or the Department of Homeland Security must enter a new appearance in each case, even if they were the practitioner of record at the time that discipline was imposed. See Chapter 2.1(b) (Entering an Appearance as the Practitioner of Record).

This page intentionally left blank.

Chapter 11 Forms

11.1 Forms Generally

There is an official form that must be used to:

- Appear as a practitioner of record. See Chapter 2.1(b) (Entering an Appearance as the Practitioner of Record)

- Disclose document assistance through limited appearance. See Chapter 2.1(c) (Limited Appearance for Document Assistance)

- Report a change of address. See Chapter 2.2(c) (Address Obligations)

- Request most kinds of relief. See 8 C.F.R. parts 299, 1299

- File an appeal. See Chapter 6 (Appeals of Immigration Judge Decisions)

- Request a fee waiver on appeal. See Chapter 3.4 (Filing Fees)

There is an official form that should be used to:

- File a practitioner or recognized organization complaint. See Chapter 10.5 (Filing a Complaint)

There is no official form to:

- File a motion. See Chapter 5.2(b) (Form)

- File a FOIA request. See Chapter 12 (Requesting Records)

11.2 Obtaining Blank Forms

(a) Identifying EOIR Forms — Many forms used by the Executive Office for Immigration Review (EOIR) do not appear in the regulations. The EOIR forms most commonly used by the public are identified in this manual. See Appendix D (Forms). Form names and numbers can be obtained from the immigration courts and the Clerk's Office of the Board of Immigration Appeals. See Appendix A (Directory).

(b) Obtaining EOIR Forms — Appendix D (Forms) contains a list of frequently requested forms and information on where to obtain them. In general, EOIR forms are available from the following sources:

- The EOIR website

- The immigration courts

- The Clerk's Office of the Board of Immigration Appeals

- Certain Government Printing Office Bookstores

Parties should be sure to use the most recent version of each form, which will be available from the sources listed above.

(c) Obtaining DHS Forms — In general, DHS forms are available at www.uscis.gov.

(d) Photocopied Forms — Photocopies of blank EOIR forms may be used, provided that they are an accurate duplication of the government-issued form and are printed on the correct size and stock of paper. See 8 C.F.R. §§ 299.4(a), 1299.1. The filing party is responsible for the accuracy and legibility of the form. The paper used to photocopy the form should also comply with Chapter 3.3(c)(5) (Paper size and document quality). The most recent version of the form *must be used* and is available from the sources listed in subsection (b), above.

For the forms listed in subsection (f), below, the use of colored paper is strongly encouraged, but not required.

(e) Computer-Generated Forms — Computer-generated versions of EOIR forms may be used, provided that they are an accurate duplication of the government-issued form and are printed on the correct size and stock of paper. See 8 C.F.R. §§ 299.4(a), 1299.1. The filing party is responsible for the accuracy and legibility of the form. The paper used to photocopy the form should also comply with Chapter 3.3(c)(5) (Paper size and document quality). The most recent version of the form *must be used* and is available from the sources listed in subsection (b), above.

For the forms listed in subsection (f), below, when filing a paper form, the use of colored paper is strongly encouraged, but not required.

(f) Form Colors — Forms are no longer required to be filed on paper of a specific color. However, the use of colored paper for the forms listed below is strongly encouraged. Any submission that is not a form must be on white paper.

blue — EOIR-26 (Notice of Appeal / Immigration Judge Decision)

tan — EOIR-26A (Appeal Fee Waiver Request)

yellow — EOIR-27 (Notice of Appearance before the Board of Immigration Appeals)

green — EOIR-28 (Notice of Appearance before the Immigration Court)

pink — EOIR-29 (Notice of Appeal / DHS decision)

pink — EOIR-33/BIA (Change of Address / Board of Immigration Appeals)

blue — EOIR-33/IC (Change of Address / Immigration Court)

11.3   Submitting Completed Forms

Completed forms must comply with the signature requirements in Chapter 3.3(b) (Signatures). No form requiring an ink signature will be considered complete if submitted with a digital or electronic signature. In all instances, the filing party must comply with the form instructions.

11.4   Additional Information

For further information on filing requirements, see Chapter 3 (Filing with the Immigration Court). See also Chapters 5 (Motions before the Immigration Court), 6 (Appeals of Immigration Judge Decisions), 8 (Stays), 9 (Detention and Bond), 10 (Discipline of Practitioners), 12 (Requesting Records).

This page intentionally left blank.

Chapter 12 Requesting Records

12.1 Generally

The Freedom of Information Act (FOIA) provides the public with access to federal agency records, with certain exceptions. See 5 U.S.C. § 552. The Executive Office for Immigration Review, Office of the General Counsel, FOIA Service Center responds to FOIA requests for immigration court records. See Appendix A (Directory).

12.2 Requests

For detailed guidance on how to file a FOIA request, individuals requesting information under the Freedom of Information Act should consult the EOIR website or contact the EOIR FOIA Service Center. See Appendix A (Directory). General guidelines are as follows.

(a) Who May File

(1) Parties

(A) Inspecting the record — Parties to an immigration court proceeding and their practitioners of record may inspect the official record of proceedings. A FOIA request is not required. Inspection by prior arrangement with court staff is strongly recommended to ensure that the official record is immediately available. Individual immigration courts can be reached by using the following email model: "EOIR.xyz.ROP.Requests@usdoj.gov" where the "xyz" represents the relevant immigration court's three-letter code. See Appendix Q (Immigration Court Three Letter Codes). Parties may review all portions of the record that are not prohibited (e.g., classified information, documents under a protective order). EOIR prohibits the removal of official records by parties or other persons from EOIR-controlled space.

(B) Obtaining copies of the record — The immigration courts will provide copies of the official record of proceedings to parties and their practitioners of record upon request. A FOIA request is not required. Parties may obtain a copy of all portions of the record that are not prohibited to the party (e.g., classified information, documents under a protective order). Requests for copies of the official record of proceedings may be made to the immigration courts in person, by mail, or via email. See email model above in the ICPM, Chapter 12.2(a)(1)(A). See Chapter 1.5(c) (Records). The immigration courts do not provide self-service copying.

(2) Non-parties — Persons who are not a party to a proceeding before an immigration court must file a FOIA request with the EOIR Office of the General Counsel if they wish to see or obtain copies of the record of proceedings. See subsection (b), below.

(b) How to File

(1) Form — FOIA requests must be made in writing. See 28 C.F.R. § 16.1 et seq. Although the Executive Office for Immigration Review (EOIR) does not have an official form for filing FOIA requests, the Form EOIR-59, Certification and Release of Records, can be used in conjunction with a FOIA request when requesting third party information. See Appendix D (Forms). The Department of Homeland Security Freedom of Information/Privacy Act Request (Form G-639) should not be used to file such requests. For information on where to file a FOIA request, contact the EOIR FOIA Service Center. See Appendix A (Directory).

(2) Information required — Requests should thoroughly describe the records sought and include as much identifying information as possible regarding names, dates, subject matter, and location of proceedings. For example, if a request pertains to a respondent in removal proceedings, the request should contain the full name and A-number of that respondent. The more precise and comprehensive the information provided in the FOIA request, the better and more expeditiously the request can be processed.

(3) Fee — No fee is required to file a FOIA request, but fees may be charged to locate, review, and reproduce records. See 28 C.F.R. § 16.10(c).

(4) Processing times — Processing times for FOIA requests vary depending on the nature of the request and the location of the records.

(c) When to File

(1) Timing — A FOIA request should be filed as soon as possible, especially when a party is facing a filing deadline.

(2) Effect on filing deadlines — Parties should not delay the filing of an application, motion, brief, appeal, or other document while awaiting a response to a FOIA request. Non-receipt of materials requested pursuant to FOIA does *not* excuse a party's failure to meet a filing deadline.

(d) Limitations

(1) Statutory exemptions — Certain information in agency records, such as classified material and information that would cause a clearly unwarranted invasion of personal privacy, is exempted from release under FOIA. See 5 U.S.C. § 552(b)(1)-(9). Where appropriate, such information is redacted (i.e., removed or cut out), and a copy of the redacted record is provided to the requesting party. If material is redacted, the reasons for the redaction are indicated.

(2) Agency's duty — The FOIA statute does not require the Executive Office for Immigration Review, its Office of the General Counsel, or the immigration courts to perform legal research, nor does it entitle the requesting person to copies of documents that are available for sale or on the internet.

(3) Subject's consent — When a FOIA request seeks information that is exempt from disclosure on the grounds of personal privacy, the subject of the record must consent in writing to the release of the information.

12.3 Denials

If a FOIA request is denied, either in whole or in part, the requesting party may appeal the decision to the Office of Information and Privacy, Department of Justice. Information on how to appeal a denial of a FOIA request is available on the Office of Information and Privacy website at www.justice.gov/oip. The rules regarding FOIA appeals can be found at 28 C.F.R. § 16.9.

This page intentionally left blank.

Chapter 13 Public Input

13.1 Generally

(a) Practice Manual — The Executive Office for Immigration Review welcomes and encourages the public to provide comments on the Practice Manual. In particular, the public is encouraged to identify errors or ambiguities in the text and to propose revisions for future editions.

Correspondence regarding the Practice Manual should be addressed to:

United States Department of Justice
Executive Office for Immigration Review
Office of the Chief Immigration Judge
5107 Leesburg Pike, 18th Floor
Falls Church, VA 22041

The public is asked not to combine comments regarding the Practice Manual with other inquiries, including inquiries regarding specific matters pending before the immigration courts.

(b) Regulations and Published Rules — Periodically, EOIR issues new regulations. New regulations are published in the *Federal Register*, in most law libraries, and in many public libraries. The public is encouraged to submit comments on regulations as instructions provide in each relevant publication.

This page intentionally left blank.

Index

Citation Index

A separate Word Index precedes this index.

Made in the USA
Monee, IL
03 November 2024

07477821-a59f-414c-bb31-153e28b00c93R01